Those Were the Days
Leicestershire
in the Forties, Fifties and Sixties

David Bell

COUNTRYSIDE BOOKS
Newbury, Berkshire

First published 2001
© David Bell 2001

COUNTRYSIDE BOOKS
3 Catherine Road
Newbury, Berkshire

To view our complete range of books,
please visit us at
www.countrysidebooks.co.uk

ISBN 1 85306 698 2

For my sister, Joan

Designed by K.D.P., Kingsclere
Produced through MRM Associates Ltd., Reading
Typeset by Techniset Typesetters, Newton-le-Willows
Printed by Woolnough Bookbinding Ltd., Irthlingborough

CONTENTS

INTRODUCTION

This book is about life in Leicestershire during the years 1939 to 1969. After I appealed for memories of this period, via the local newspapers and local radio, I was contacted by people from all parts of the county. By integrating their memories with my own, I hope I have created a book that will bring back a flavour of the times.

Margaret Sparrow, nee Margaret Hoden, grew up in the village of Stanton-under-Bardon, in north-west Leicestershire. Her accounts of her father joining the local Home Guard and of the various evacuees who came to live in her home are both humorous and poignant. From the opposite end of the county, Frank Bingley, of Gumley, near Market Harborough, contributes a nostalgic and evocative account of growing up in a farming community in the 1950s, describing a rural way of life that is fast disappearing.

Jean Philps, nee Orton, still lives in Sharnford, the village where she was raised, in the south of the county. Her reminiscences of life at home, at school and at church make her early life in Sharnford sound idyllic. Anne Silins now lives in Canada, but memories of her childhood in Appleby Magna – she was then Anne Bates – are as vivid as ever. While her years there were very happy, her stories of going to a new school in Ashby-de-la-Zouch in the 1940s provide us with a timely reminder that not everything in the 'Good Old Days' was as pleasant as we sometimes claim.

My own contributions come from Melton Mowbray, where I went to my junior school (all boys – boo!) in the 1940s, and to the grammar school (co-ed – hurray!) in the 1950s, before teaching in the town and raising my own family there in the 1960s.

Kay Moon was a city girl, growing up in the Spinney Hills area of Leicester. She remembers going to the Palais de Danse, where she almost danced with a future international singing star. Happy memories of whirling to the music of the Danny Rogers Orchestra at the De Montfort Hall are recalled by Ann Jones of Kirby Muxloe, who also describes just how much effort went into creating the beehive hairstyle favoured by girls in the late Fifties. It is not surprising that the De Montfort Hall also features strongly in the memories of Malcolm O'Shea, since his father was the entertainments manager there, booking such stars as Mario Lanza, Frank Sinatra and Danny Kaye, as well as Sixties groups including the Beatles and Rolling Stones.

The three decades of the period were very different. The Forties were of course the years of the war, and of post-war austerity. The Sixties have become known as a time of excitement, of free love, flower power, of the younger generation throwing off the shackles of the past, in that memorable phrase, 'If you can remember the Sixties, you weren't really there.' The intervening Fifties are often written off as a mere time of transition between the hardship of the Forties and the Swinging Sixties, but for some of us who were in our teens then, 'those were the days'.

Of course, events didn't fit neatly into the decades of the calendar. Rationing – that abiding feature of the Forties – went on into the early Fifties. The Swinging Sixties actually began in 1957 or 1958. I know – I was there! However, to keep things simple, the first few chapters of the book look at the Forties, Fifties and Sixties as if they really were distinct decades. The rest of the book takes an overall look at different aspects of life – transport, schools, shopping, taking a bath, how we spent our leisure time, the comics we read and the sweets we ate – throughout the whole period. I hope that *Those Were The Days – Leicestershire* will remind people of that fascinating journey from one world to another.

David Bell

CHAPTER ONE
GAS MASKS AND AIR RAIDS

The first half of the Forties covers the war period, and was a time of rationing and shortages, though to those of us who were children at the time, we were not really aware of it. We went to school, played out in the street, and lived our lives oblivious to the hardships that our parents were putting up with. It's true that some of our friends had dads who were away fighting in the army, but that just seemed a fact of life.

We did sometimes see the German bomber planes in the sky, and we would be told to shelter under the table or under the stairs 'in case the windows come in'. Our next-door neighbours had an Anderson shelter at the bottom of their garden, but my family only tried using it once. On hearing a siren one night, my parents picked me up and went into the shelter with our neighbours. They waited for hours but heard nothing more. Eventually, my father was sent out to investigate, and he discovered that the siren that had sent them into the shelter had been, in fact, the all-clear. 'In future, if we've got to go then we'll go in our beds,' he decided and that was that.

Leicestershire had its share of bombs, particularly in Leicester, where the air raids of 19th November 1940 killed 108 people. Holwell Ironworks, where my dad worked, made munitions during the war and it did have three bombing raids, but Leicestershire had nothing on the scale of Coventry, eight miles from the Leicestershire county boundary. We would see the planes heading for that city crossing the Leicestershire skies, and would later see the glow from the bombing lighting up the horizon to the south-east.

The author, aged three.

Those fathers who were not in the forces would often be members of the Home Guard. Margaret Sparrow (nee Hoden) grew up in Stanton-under-Bardon, near Coalville, and recalls, 'The Home Guard was started about 1940. The very first meeting was held one Sunday morning in the field at the back of our house. About twenty men turned up, including my dad. They were drilled and marched up and down armed with brush handles, garden rakes, spades and hoes, carried on their shoulders like rifles. Mr Johnson, who had been a sergeant in the first war, was giving the orders. In the village we had an ARP unit as well. My grandfather was a member of this. Their headquarters were in the old school, just across the road from where I lived. The Home

7

Bert Hoden was in the Stanton Home Guard.
(Margaret Sparrow)

Not a hair out of place

For a iperfect set, whetlier you are blond or brunette, use a few drops of non-sticky, quick-drying Amami Wave Set. Two kinds: AMAMI STANDARD and AMAMI SPIRITOUS.

AMAMI WAVE SET

10½d. and 2/1½d. per bottle. Inclusive of Purchase Tax.

'Friday night is Amami night' was the slogan many women will remember.

Guard used the same building. The ARP was called out when the siren was sounded. Their job was to patrol the village in case a bomb was dropped, and to get people to a safe place. They had to make sure that no lights were showing from the house windows at night. If there were, they would shout, "Put that light out!" With the war came all the safety precautions: sand bags at the door, sticky tape on the windows to stop the glass falling out in case of an explosion from a bomb, and blackout curtains at the windows so that the light did not show outside. It made everywhere very depressing.

'We did get two bombs very near the village on the night that Coventry was bombed. The next day, I can remember standing at the top of the village as it was still burning and I could see smoke from the fire. Our air raid shelter was under the stairs and we spent two nights there. That was my mother and me, my gran, four evacuee children and their mother. Quite a crowd in such a small place!'

Anne Silins (nee Bates) says of her school in Ashby-de-la-Zouch, 'When I started, I was issued with a small square cardboard box. I was completely at a loss to know what to do with it, until I was told to go to the school secretary's office. She told me it was a gas mask, and told me how to put it on. At playtime, we would practise putting on the gas masks. We would shout at each other, running round with outstretched arms, blowing hard to see who could make the rudest sound as the air was forced out past our cheeks. The celluloid eyepiece steamed up and then we bumped into one another. I proudly took mine back and forward each day, but the cardboard boxes wore out and

Rinso would save the day when 'Peg' came home on leave from the factory!

we were given metal cylinders. There was a string attached so that we could hang it round our necks, but then the boys would grab it, giving us a jolt. I wore mine hanging on my shoulder, but one day a boy on the bus grabbed it and tossed it out of the window. When I told my family, all grandad said was, "You'd just better hope Hitler doesn't launch a gas attack today". Luckily the gas mask survived the fall, and because my name was painted on it, someone in the village found it and it was returned to me. I was very relieved.'

Margaret Sparrow also remembers the dreaded gas masks. 'Gas masks were issued to everyone in the village. Babies had a special one like a large bag that they were put into; it had an air pump that was operated by hand all the time they were in it. Later on another piece was added to the end of the mask, in case of a mustard gas attack. We had gas mask drill every morning after assembly at school. First we had to keep them on for five minutes, then ten and up to half an hour. I hated it. My face would get all hot and the see-through panel at the front would get all steamed up. School nature walks were

'Aunty' Peg, who came for three days and stayed for three years.

not the same any more as it was not safe to go far from the school in case of an air raid. There was a special drill for when we were out in the fields. If there was a siren warning, a teacher blew a whistle. All the children had to scatter and find a space, lie down on the ground and put their hands over their ears. I didn't like this as I was afraid of spiders and there always seemed to be a lot in the grass where I was.'

Like Stanton-under-Bardon, the village of Kirby Muxloe had a bomb dropped on it. Anne Jones writes, 'To a four-year-old child, the outbreak of war in Kirby Muxloe registered little until in 1941 when the village was bombed. This event coincided with the departure of many fathers into the services. Some did not return until after the war, a few did not return at all. Blackout curtains, dark streets, the drone of aircraft in the night, sparse rations and hand-me-down clothes seemed just normal life since we had nothing else with which to compare it.'

Although fathers were going away, the war also meant that many households took in new guests. One new member of our family was a young lady named Peggy Andrews, or Aunty Peg as I called her. She was not a real aunty – not a relative at all, in fact – but in those days no child would refer to a grown-up by his or her Christian name, even if that grown-up was only nineteen, so any adult friend of the family had an honorary *aunty* or *uncle* added to their name. Aunty Peg first came into our lives in 1943, when I was four. A billeting officer knocked on the door of our house in Melton Mowbray and asked my mum if she would take in a young lady from the north, who had been drafted to work as a civilian shorthand typist at the Old Dalby army ordnance depot. Mum said that she didn't want to take in a lodger as she'd tried it before and it hadn't worked out well. The nineteen-year-old girl who was with the officer began to cry and mum's heart melted. 'Well,' she said, 'she can stay for three days while she looks around for somewhere more permanent.' The girl, Peggy Andrews, dried her eyes and came to stay. In fact, she came for three days and stayed for over three years!

Aunty Peg spoiled me rotten. In the evening she would tiptoe upstairs. 'I know where you're going,' mum would say. 'No, I'm just nipping up to my room for something,' Peg would reply untruthfully. Actually, she would come up to my room and read to me. On one occasion when I was five, Aunty Peg and her friend Jean Jackson ('Aunty' Jean to me, of course) took me to the fair being held in the playclose in Melton. I begged to go on the dodgems and Aunty Peg agreed, but when our car hit another, my face hit the steering wheel. When I developed a real black eye, Peg became very worried and daren't take me home. She and Jean walked me round town for

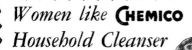

Many household products were scarce in wartime.

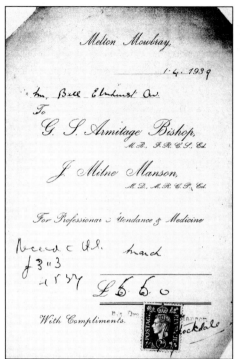

*The doctor's bills for the births of the author in 1939
and his sister Joan in 1943 – a bargain
at three guineas!*

two and a half hours, hoping that my eye would go down. Eventually, she gave up and took me back to Elmhurst Avenue, dreading what my mother would say. Apparently mum took one look at my black eye and burst out laughing!

A more common form of lodgers during this period were evacuees, children who had been sent into rural Leicestershire to avoid the bombing in their home cities. Margaret Sparrow remembers them well. 'I was seven years old when the war started and my mother was a member of the WVS. She had quite a busy time with the distribution of the evacuees when they arrived in the village. The old school house was the centre where they were assembled after arriving by bus. Then they were taken out to the homes that had been found for them with families in the village. Anyone who had a spare room would

The three Birmingham evacuees and (front) Margaret Hoden. (Margaret Sparrow)

have someone to live with them, unless they had a very good excuse.

'Three girls from Birmingham were the first to come to live with us. They had to go to our school, along with other evacuees in the village. The hall at the school was turned into a classroom for the new children, which meant we could not have dancing any more. Also we now had to sit three to a desk, instead of two. We had to share our books with these strange new pupils, endure new teachers that were not at all nice, and hear a language that was very different to our own. I had to share my bedroom with three strangers, whether I liked it or not. This was hard for me because I never had any brothers or sisters. We got on well together really, but they were homesick and wanted to go home.

'Often, my mum would be left with those evacuees that no one else wanted. Very late one night, after the Birmingham girls had gone home, mum had been out all day taking more evacuees to their allotted homes. When she had finished there was still a woman with a baby, so they had to come to live with us. The 14-month-old baby, named David, had not been changed out of his nappy or fed properly from the time they had left their home that morning. His bottom was so sore that he was not able to go in a bath for a week, until it had healed up. He learned to walk while he was with us and I spent a lot of time looking after him. His mother didn't really want him, and sometime after they left, she wrote to ask my parents if they would adopt him but they didn't take up her offer.

'Another time, we had a woman and four children staying with us. While they were here, a really funny thing happened. The five of them lived in the front room of the house, which had been turned into a bed-sitting room. They bought their own food, but used our kitchen to cook it. Bread was still on ration, so we could only get so much per person per week. Because our toilet was outside, they had to use a large pot under the bed, but they never emptied it until it was full to the top. One day the children were playing throwing a loaf of bread over the bed, when it fell into the full pot. The woman fished it out and dried it in front of the fire, then made them eat it for their tea! That day I was going to have my tea with them, but luckily I always took my own food with me. Thank goodness for rationing. The woman was a heavy smoker, and because cigarettes were on ration, you could only get one packet at a time from the shop. She would send one of the children to say they were for my dad. Mother asked them to move on after they set fire to the rug and the curtains. I was glad to see them go, as I often got the blame for things they had done.'

CHAPTER TWO
1945-1950: AFTER THE WAR

After the war, men began to come home, but for some people this was a mixed blessing. Obviously, the adult members of the family were overjoyed to welcome back their sons, brothers and husbands, but for the younger children the return of a father they'd never seen meant a stranger was entering their life.

Anne Jones comments, 'Five years of being the eldest child of three in what was in essence a one-parent family came to an abrupt halt with the arrival home of the masculine head-of-the-household. My youngest brother – then aged five – had never seen his father. No bonding, as deemed so important today, had taken place and has never done so in all the years since. In fact there seemed to be a mutual resentment between them. This situation must have been mirrored in thousands of families across the land.'

In 1945, many communities – towns, villages and cities – held street parties to celebrate VE Day in May and VJ Day in September. In my own street in Melton Mowbray, we had a fancy dress parade

We could begin to think about our homes and surroundings again in 1946.

and a party with trestle tables down the middle of the street. In the evening, we went into the army camp behind our houses for further entertainment. On one of these occasions (probably VJ Day), the soldiers took all the children to see a special horse, a big white one. We were all lifted on and off this horse and told that we would be able to tell our grandchildren that we had sat on the horse belonging to a German general named Rommel.

Pat Hall grew up in Leicester, and recalls the VE Day celebrations in King Richard's Road. 'A bonfire was lit in the middle of the road, and when it was dying down, people brought all the doors off the outside loos and threw them on to keep the fires going,' she tells me, adding, 'and the heat melted the road!'

Margaret Sparrow remembers the street parties too, and comments that they were an occasion for some rivalry. 'Some trestle tables were borrowed and set up along the street. There had always been a division in Stanton between the top-enders, where I lived, and the bottom-enders, so there was keen competition as to who was having the best food. The mums made the sandwiches and cakes while the dads organised the games. We each had to

Our VE Day fancy dress parade in Elmhurst Avenue,
Melton Mowbray.

Another VE Day parade, this one at Stanton-under-Bardon. (Margaret Sparrow)

THE DAILY ROUND

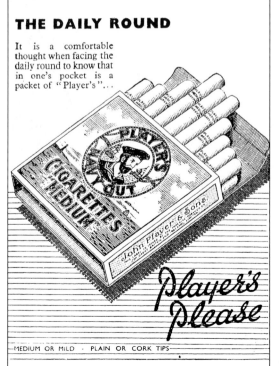

It is a comfortable thought when facing the daily round to know that in one's pocket is a packet of "Player's"...

PLAYER'S NAVY CUT CIGARETTES MEDIUM

John Player & Sons

Player's Please

MEDIUM OR MILD · PLAIN OR CORK TIPS

take our own cup, plate and chair.'

Birthday parties also started becoming a family event after the war ended. The food was always sandwiches followed by jelly and blancmange, often turned out of a mould in the shape of a rabbit. Mums would insist that all the sandwiches must be eaten before the sweet things were served. In fact, there were mums who would insist that a slice of bread and butter

Cigarettes had got many people through the war and we were still being told how good they were for us.

must be eaten *with* the jelly. Exotic fruits were gradually coming back; many is the child who stared at a banana and wondered how you got to the inside of it. I remember the very first banana my mum obtained after the war. It was still rather green so she put it onto the windowsill of the front room to ripen in the sun, only to be accused by a banana-less jealous neighbour of 'showing off'! Not everyone had to wait until peacetime to have a party. Anne Jones comments that while most of her friends had very frugal parties, she was luckier in that respect. 'I was fortunate because my father was stationed in Iceland for most of the war, and having access to the American PX on the island, he was able to send us such luxuries as real jellies, maple syrup, cowboy gauntlets, sheepskin rugs and, best of all, chocolate cream biscuits. The occasional tin of peaches, ham or meat-paste was hoarded for special occasions, and even now – over 50 years on – contemporaries of mine still remember these treats from being invited to my birthday parties.'

One aspect of life that did change in the second half of the decade was that people were now able to go away on holiday. Leicestershire is about as far from the sea as it is possible to get, so a visit to the seaside was eagerly

Rationing went on, but parties and special occasions brought out the hoarded goodies – this was Boxing Day at Grandma Wainer's in 1948.

With the end of the war,
our thoughts could turn to holidays
once more. This advertisement
was from 1949.

anticipated. Many Leicestershire folk looked to the east coast for their seaside trips, especially to Skegness – always known as Skeggy – and Mablethorpe. It was even said that, during the July fortnight when the Leicestershire factories shut down, there were so many Leicester folk in Skegness that more copies of the *Leicester Mercury* were sold in Skeggy than back in Leicester. If you were prepared to go even further to get somewhere more exotic, there was also Great Yarmouth or Cromer.

When I was about seven, my mum, my little sister Joan and I went on a Skegness holiday with my Aunty Mary (no relation – just a friend of the family) and her son Brian. Brian was about the same age as Joan. Neither my dad nor Aunty Mary's husband came with us. For many years, I thought the reason my dad didn't come on holiday with us was because he wouldn't leave his chrysanthemums (he was a keen gardener), but my sister has recently pointed out the real reason – men in those days didn't get a paid holiday and dad couldn't afford to take the time off work. He was only earning £2/5/- a week, and 15s of this went on the rent. Whenever we went on holiday, all the neighbours would give my sister and me two shillings (or even half a crown) for spending money. The only commitment was to bring each of them a stick of rock back. Of course, when the neighbours went away, my own parents would give each of their children two shillings to spend.

In Skegness, we stayed at a boarding house owned by a very fierce lady named Mrs Murphy. As soon as we arrived, she told the two mums that the three

The author, sister Joan and Mum at Skeggy in 1946.

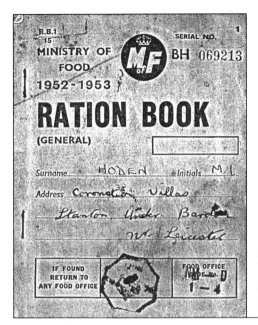

Margaret Hoden's ration book for 1952-3 shows how rationing still dominated our post-war lives. (Margaret Sparrow)

children must be kept under strict supervision, as she had a middle-aged couple staying who had no children and therefore they wouldn't want to hear children about the place. Actually this wasn't true; they took me out on the boating lake some days. I think perhaps that Mrs Murphy disapproved of us being a party of two women and three children with no men present. We spent all day and every day on the beach, as we were not allowed to stay in the boarding house during the daytime. I suspect mum and Aunty Mary found things a bit fraught and future holidays were taken in a caravan.

They were all *dad-less* holidays though. The first holiday I can remember where dad came with us was in 1948 when we went to stay with his brother and family in Denham, near Uxbridge. This was the year of the Olympics and we all went up to Windsor to see the athlete run past with the Olympic torch. The streets were lined with people and we stood for ages waiting. Just before the man came into sight, one unfortunate lady fainted and had to be taken to the back of the crowd. She came round only to discover that she had missed the great event. While at Denham, we also used to go into London, and I was able to collect autographs from the many Olympic athletes wandering about

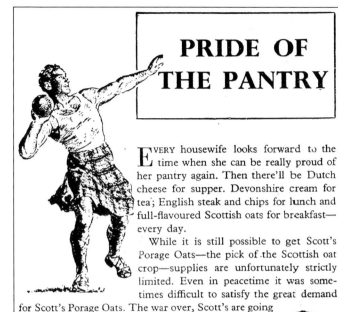

the streets. This holiday was a one-off, though, to visit relations. All our other trips were to the east coast, either to Skeggy, Great Yarmouth, or Cromer.

However, people from the north-west of the county looked to all the fun of Blackpool as their chosen destination. Margaret Sparrow recalls: 'In 1945, we were able to go away on the first holiday since the war began. In September, mum and dad took me to Blackpool. We went by train from the Central Station in Leicester. Because food was still on ration, we decided to take our own eggs with us. The two dozen eggs were packed in sawdust and carried all the way with great care! When we arrived at the station in Blackpool, we were met by a group of enterprising lads with carts and wheelbarrows, wanting 6d to carry our cases to our lodgings. There were no taxis, so we had to walk. At the boarding house, the ration books had to be handed over to the landlady so that she had our coupons for the week's food.'

As Margaret indicates, many things remained on ration after the war. This was in order to ensure a fair distribution of what food was available. As in wartime, if there had been a free market while there were still shortages, then those people with money would have been able to obtain vast quantities of what food there was, while the rest of us went without. In spite of rationing, there were always people who could get things illegally (on the 'black market'). A man in our street worked on a farm, and he could sometimes obtain extra meat if a pig had been unofficially slaughtered. Unfortunately, my dad was so scrupulously honest that he would have nothing to do with these activities. On reflection, perhaps *unfortunately* is the wrong word; we were lucky to have a dad with strong principles.

We did eke out the rations with chickens, which were reared in the back garden. Most people seemed to do the same, and as my dad was the only one in the neighbourhood with the required skills (being country reared), he was always fetched when it was time to wring their necks. I remember being both horrified and fascinated to see the dead chickens still flapping their wings. 'It's just their nerves,' people said, whatever that meant. These hens must have had special powers too since every Easter we had boiled eggs that were different colours. There would be a red one, a yellow one and a blue one. I remember my father taking me up the garden and pointing out which hen had laid which colour egg!

One year remembered by everyone who lived through it was the winter of 1947, when it froze, then snowed, then froze again. The snowdrifts were ten feet high and stayed for months, many Leicestershire villages being cut off completely. 'Fred', from Wigston reminded me that the first path you dug was not the one from the house to the front gate but a path from the back door to the WC down the garden. The hurricane lamp to keep the WC thawed was kept lit all winter. People struggled valiantly to carry on life as normal. Jean Philps recalls that Mr Pratt, the headmaster of Sharnford village school, walked along the hedgetops from his home in Broughton Astley that winter, and he never missed a day's teaching. While the adults strove to keep life safe and normal, we children enjoyed snowball fights and sledging. The snow drifts may have meant difficulty for our parents but Jean adds, 'All the children who lived at the top end of Sharnford made marvellous caves in the snowdrifts at the top of Mill Lane.'

CHAPTER THREE
THE SPIRITED FIFTIES

The Fifties began (well actually it was 1951) with the Festival of Britain celebrations, and I remember being taken to London to see the Skylon and the Dome of Discovery. There was a lot of controversy at the time, with newspaper articles querying whether these were a waste of money that could have been spent on schools or hospitals. A dome in London being a waste of money? Who says history never repeats itself!

Miner's daughter Jill Driver of Ibstock amazed me by recalling that during the 1950s, her family went to Blackpool, travelling all the way there by taxi! I still find that incredible. I thought my family was doing things the posh way when we used a taxi to take our

The Festival of Britain in 1951 seemed to signal a fresh start.

luggage and us to the bus station, but that was only 1¹/₂ miles. Margaret Sparrow adds further details of the taxi-travelling holiday-makers of north-west Leicestershire. 'In the Fifties we had many holidays in Blackpool, but we didn't go by train any more. We went by taxi! A firm in Coalville called Centax would take you all the way to Blackpool and back for £14. There were no motorways then, so the trip used to take seven hours. The cars – known as the Yellow Perils, because they were bright yellow with black roofs – would seat seven people, so we used to share with another family from the village, to help out with the fare. One year there was a mix-up with the passengers. Some people who had travelled up earlier had gone for a fortnight rather than a week, and the driver hadn't realised. They had to come back with us, so that meant ten passengers with all the luggage piled high on a roof rack. It was a real squeeze, and certainly wouldn't be legal today.'

During the Forties, very few people had a car. In my street in Melton Mowbray, there was only one car owner, a Mr Preston who had a white-collar job with the council. If my mate Maurice and I saw him backing his car

Floods in Nottingham Road, Melton in June 1953.
(Arnold Jordan)

out, we would beg a lift to the corner of the street, then walk home boasting. During the Fifties however, car ownership became more common, petrol rationing being abolished in 1950. The price of a new car at that time was less than £500, so second-hand ones could be picked up much cheaper. Petrol was only 3 shillings a gallon, but the proliferation of car ownership led to traffic congestion in Leicester. One solution tried was the building of wider roads through the city, but this only led to yet more traffic. Alf Jones of Leicester comments, 'It's a pity they did away with the trams in 1949. They're just what's needed now to get people out of their cars.'

One event of 1953 – the Coronation of Queen Elizabeth – led both to the resurrection of an old phenomenon and to a brand new one. The old one was the street parties and fancy dress parades last seen in 1945, complete with decorated houses and public buildings flying the Union Jack. What was new was the buying of television sets. Television hadn't really taken off until then, but the news that the Coronation was to be televised meant that many families went out and bought their first TV set. Everything was in black and white, of

A street party in Diseworth Street, Leicester in 1953 to celebrate the Coronation. (Kay Moon)

The living room at Home Farm, Gumley in the mid Fifties – note the early television set. (Frank Bingley)

course, with just one channel, and watched on a 9 inch screen, but we all agreed that the whole thing was a blooming marvel. Jean Philps from Sharnford reminisces, 'Grandad bought our first television for the Queen's Coronation. It was one of the first in the village and loads of people came to watch. One lady, whose son was on duty as a guardsman, shouted, "There's our Pete!" as the cameras moved down the line of soldiers in bearskins. How she could tell on such a small screen was beyond me – they all looked alike!' Like Jean's grandfather, our neighbours bought a TV set in time for the Coronation and invited us all in. Strangely, everyone drew the curtains and watched in semi-darkness in those days. In the evenings, the lights were switched off while watching television, a practice perhaps derived from going to the cinema.

The habit of sharing your television with the neighbours went on throughout the Fifties, as Frank Bingley of Gumley near Market Harborough recalls. 'Although television had been around for a number of years before I was born in 1947, very few people had a TV set. The first one I remember belonged to Sam and Kathleen Seabrook. I used to go round their house and watch it. It stood on the floor in a wood veneer case with castors on the bottom. Two doors would open to reveal the screen and control knobs, and the large speaker grille was at the bottom. When we got our own TV, it was much the same type of thing except that ours was a table top model. It was of course a 405 line model, which must have made the picture very grainy. There were normally no programmes shown during the day, only in the evenings. At about 11 pm, transmissions would cease and a voice said, "You will remember to turn the TV off, won't you?" Then would come a loud tone, and a bright spot in the middle of the screen. It was very common for people to come round in the evenings just to watch TV, but as more and more people began to get sets of their own, this practice gradually disappeared.'

Another 'invention' of the Fifties was the teenager. Before the Fifties, people left school at 14 or 15 and became mini-adults straight away. They found a job, met a sweetheart and began saving for their 'bottom drawer' so that they could get married and become like their parents. If they went out, they danced to the music of the Danny Rogers Orchestra at the De Montfort Hall, like their parents before them. In the Fifties however, teenagers discovered that

Bernice Parr's twelfth birthday party in 1951 (note the precocious couples at the front!). Bernice would soon be one of those new inventions – the teenager.

there was another way of life, different from that of their parents. Anne Jones comments, 'Fashion, as clothing coupons were phased out, swung from the *New Look* to flouncy petticoats and stiletto heels which ruined every marley tile or parquet floor. The end of the Fifties brought in beehive coiffures for the females. These were backcombed each Saturday and never touched again until the following weekend, kept in place while in bed by winding toilet paper round the head, covered with a hairnet.' We spent our money in the newly opened coffee bars, and we listened to jazz and skiffle. Some of us formed our own skiffle groups with home-made instruments, like washboards and tea-chest basses.

Suddenly, in the mid-50s, rock'n'roll arrived on the scene. I remember going to Leicester to see the film *The Blackboard Jungle*, about a tough New York school. The soundtrack of this film was provided by Bill Haley and his Comets singing *Rock Around The Clock*. This was one of the first rock'n'roll tunes we had heard. Of course, rock'n'roll didn't suddenly appear out of nowhere – it was based on the older rhythm and blues style but played with an extra loud drummer – but to the kids of the 50s, it seemed as if it had come from another

The Evergreen Party at Christmas 1956 in the Sharnford YMCA Hall. (Jean Philps)

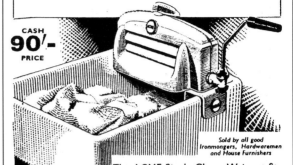
A 1955 ad that showed the average housewife was not yet enjoying a modern, labour saving kitchen.

world. There were lurid press headlines about teenagers getting up in the cinema and jiving in the aisles. In fact one of the most attractive things about this music was the universal disapproval of parents, teachers and anyone over 25. Television programmes began to appear that were designed to appeal to the teenager. Before we went out on a Saturday night, *Six-Five Special* – featuring rock'n'roll, trad jazz, skiffle, all music we regarded as our own – was an absolute must.

One group of rock'n'roll fans began to style their hair so that they had a quiff at the front, while the sides were grown long and swept back into what became known as a DA. (These initials stood for the rear part of a duck's anatomy.) These teenagers wore long colourful jackets with velvet collars, tight drainpipe trousers and shoes with thick crepe soles. Because this type of clothing – the jackets anyway – harked back to Edwardian times, the press dubbed these teenagers Teddy Boys, and again they were universally criticised for their appearance and boisterous behaviour. For some girls, having a Teddy Boy for a boyfriend was a status symbol.

Delia Bennett of Loughborough puts her memories of the Teddy Boy hero into verse:

It seems like only yesterday that rock'n'roll came to our town
Saturday night, half past seven, admission just half a crown.
The band was coming from Leicester, I knew I had to be there,
But dad refused his permission; I sulked – it just wasn't fair.
He said a rock'n'roll dance hall was not the place for his daughter;
I cried and insisted I wasn't a child, I was nearly fifteen and a quarter.
Of course, he relented and said I could go, and I was in seventh heaven!
I hugged him and kissed him, and gave my word to be home by half-past eleven.
My cousin and I spent the following week deciding what we would wear;
Between us we bought a new lipstick, and home permed each other's hair.
At last the big night was upon us; slightly nervous we walked through the door,
And joined all the other young dancers who had crowded onto the floor.
To begin with we danced with each other, and then sat down for a while,
When suddenly someone took hold of my hand. 'Come on,' he said with a smile,
'I'll show you the steps, just follow me,' and he swung me round and around.
Laughing and breathless, I followed his lead, my feet hardly touching the ground.
Even now I remember that modern young man with the drainpipes and Tony Curtis hair,
My very first rock'n'roll partner, quite handsome and so debonair.
At school, the following Monday, I could hardly disguise my real joy
When I told all the girls in the Upper Fifth form I had danced with a real Teddy Boy.

For other girls like Stella James, taking home a Teddy Boy was a problem. She writes, 'I left school in 1955, and I got my first job as an office junior at Wolsey Ltd in King Street, Leicester. It was there I met my husband, Colin "Jesse" James. Colin came from Kilby Bridge and he was a Teddy Boy. I was worried about my parents' opinion of him, so he got a haircut and put on his best suit. They liked him anyway.'

Not everything in the Fifties was looking forward. In some areas the outlook was positively reactionary. In 1953, the BBC decided that it was impossible for anyone to take seriously any news read by a female newsreader. It was obvious that only men had the gravitas to deal with such subjects! When I did a year's pre-college teaching in 1957-58, I was surprised to find that there were separate pay scales for men and women teachers, with women being paid about 20% less than their male colleagues. According to Molly Carter of Oadby, women in local footwear and knitwear industries 'were paid just half the wages of men doing the same job.'

CHAPTER FOUR
THOSE SWINGING SIXTIES

The Sixties – which later became known as the Swinging Sixties – was a time of great changes, particularly in the area of personal relationships. The advent of the contraceptive pill meant that young people could now enjoy sex without the fear of 'getting into trouble' (ie conceiving a baby). Actually the later Fifties had been a time when young couples had made love, but the Sixties did away with the deceit and secrecy involved (or perhaps it was discretion that enabled our elders to pretend it wasn't happening). In the Sixties though, people were much more honest and open in their relationships. As Bob Dylan sang, 'The times they are a-changing.'

Anne Jones of Kirby Muxloe recalls, 'The wartime babies were coming into their own at this stage. Jobs were more plentiful, and wages and conditions were improving. Expectations of a better lifestyle were higher with young couples buying houses and cars, and even washing machines! The main horror in the back of everyone's mind was the prospect of atomic warfare, creating the beginning of the *must-have-now* and *do-it-now* brigade, just in case there would be no time in the future. National Service ceased in 1960, and despite the Korean War and Suez Crisis the militarism of the earlier part of the century had receded. Instead, assassinations seemed to impinge on our senses, especially those of J.F. Kennedy, Martin Luther King and Robert Kennedy. America no longer seemed so far away, foreign travel became more available and people began to spread their wings. Fashions changed dramatically yet again, with mini-skirts heralding the advent of tights, a boon indeed for women. Men wore flared trousers and jackets with nipped-in waists. This was indeed the age of Aquarius.'

*Frank Bingley
aged 14 in 1961.
(Frank Bingley)*

When the Beatles came along, boys began to want to wear their hair longer. This was a problem if your local barber was one of the old-fashioned sort. Frank Bingley had some difficulty with the mobile barber who used to come to Gumley. 'The village barber was Tommy Partridge who was summoned periodically to cut the family's hair. My two brothers and I, along with other boys, all dreaded this day! Tommy only knew one style – short back and sides. He would have a pair of hand operated shears, and would swiftly run them from the base of the boys' necks to almost the top of their heads, all the way round. When he'd finished, we were left with a small tuft at the top, and when we got to school the next day, everyone would laugh! By the 1960s, as we got older and the Beatle hairstyles became the fashion, we got bolder in our attempts at stopping him. I always remember Andrew Seabrook, my cousin, saying to him, "The trouble with you, Tommy Partridge, is that when you get a pair of shears in your hands, you go berserk!" By the time I reached fourteen, I'd got it worked out, that it was better to cycle the five miles into Harborough periodically, and spend half-a-crown getting my hair cut the way I wanted it.'

Things were changing in schools too. One of the biggest events in Leicestershire in the 1960s was the introduction of the Leicestershire Plan (sometimes known as the Mason plan) which affected every child and parent in the county. In the 1950s, every eleven year old in the county's junior schools took an exam – the 11+, known in Leicestershire as the QESS – to decide whether he or she would go to a grammar school or secondary modern school. It was always a bit of a lottery, and depended on where and when you took the exam. My junior school was a large single-sex town school, and we spent a year (1949-50) practising for the impending test. It dominated the whole year. We practised in class, and were even encouraged to buy books of 11+ intelligence tests to work through at home. We took the exam in our own school, whereas children from the smaller schools had to come to us to sit it. Brian MacNeil who was a pupil at the town Roman Catholic school was marched down the road with his fellow students and thus sat the 11+ in a strange environment. Unlike us, he'd had no preparation for this. It was not surprising that my school usually obtained more than its expected share of 11+ passes. The county as a whole accepted 20-25% of children into the grammar schools, but – because we were ruthlessly trained to pass it – my school averaged about 30-35% passing.

Geography was not the only anomaly. Because, at the age of eleven, girls were more academic than boys, setting a straight pass mark would have meant the grammar school intake would have had more girls than boys. The balance between the sexes was achieved by setting one pass mark for boys and a different – higher – one for girls. This meant that some boys who were selected for the grammar school got there on a lower pass mark than girls who were deemed to have 'failed'. This was a well kept secret at the time (I can imagine what parents would have thought about it), and I only discovered it myself when I became a teacher.

However, in the late 1950s, the director of education for Leicestershire, Stuart Mason, issued his plan for the reorganisation of secondary education. This involved abolishing the 11+ exam, and letting all children go to a comprehensive high school from the age of 11 to 14, and then to an upper school at 14. The county's old grammar schools became upper schools, and the secondary moderns became high schools. Initially, because the school leaving age was 15, parents had to choose whether their children should go to the upper school (they had to undertake that they would stay on until 16, the age at which they could sit the O levels). If they wanted the children to leave at 15, then they remained in the high school for an extra year. In some areas of the county, 100% of children were opting to go to 16, and when the school leaving age was raised to 16, then all children transferred to the upper school at 14, and remained there until they were 16 or 18.

This new system was introduced into two areas of the county in 1957, and the whole county was using it by 1969. This meant that Leicestershire was the first education authority to have a completely comprehensive system, somewhat surprising in a rural county run by a Conservative council. It was ironic that the city of Leicester, which ran its own education system, wanted nothing to do with the Mason plan and clung onto its grammar schools for many years. Unlike the rest of the country, we had Conservative county councillors boasting of their progressive comprehensive system, and city councillors – many of them Labour – fighting to resist the same plan. Leicestershire was always a unique place!

The abolition of the 11+ meant that primary schools became much more

Melton Grammar School. The Mason Plan in the Sixties
replaced grammar schools with comprehensive Upper schools.

friendly and relaxed places to learn. Phyllis Morgan taught at a school in Loughborough and remembers the changes in teaching methods. 'It was like a breath of fresh air. Learning became much more individual, less class-based. Children could learn at their own pace, the slower ones taking their time without feeling pressured, while the more able children could soar ahead, no longer being held back. We didn't have to separate the children into As, Bs and Cs at six or seven; they could work in mixed ability groups for many lessons, while in Maths and English they could work individually or with a partner of similar skill. The curriculum became much broader, with more time to introduce them to music, art, creative writing and dance. It is not true that the basics of number and language skills were neglected, no matter what people say now. In the schools where I taught, they gained a great deal more understanding of how Maths worked, whereas in the former system they simply learned to calculate with no understanding.'

Not all teachers agreed. John Brooks comments, 'Teaching became much harder work in the 1960s, and I looked back to the old methods of learning tables and kids being taught as a whole class with nostalgia!'

One area where Leicestershire – or in this case the city of Leicester – had a first was in traffic management. By the early Sixties, Leicester's traffic had increased greatly and control of it was taking up a disproportionate amount of police time. In 1961, Leicester became the first area to employ traffic wardens – six men and six women. At first they were used solely for making sure cars were parked legally, but four years later their powers were extended to being able to control and direct traffic. Not all motorists would agree that being the first city to use traffic wardens is a proud boast for Leicester, but at least it did free up the police officers to concentrate on other more important duties.

CHAPTER FIVE
TAKING A BATH

Margaret Hoden remembers the problems associated with taking a bath in her home in Stanton-under-Bardon. 'Bath night or bath afternoon had to be well planned. First the copper in the corner of the kitchen had to be filled with cold water from the pump over the sink. This water came from the well in the back yard. The copper had to be lit in plenty of time for it to hot up. If the bathtime was on Saturday afternoon, my father had to go next door to my grandparents' house while mum and me had our baths. He would listen to the football match on the wireless with grandpa.

'The bath was put in front of the fireplace in the living room, and then all the water had to be carried from the kitchen in buckets – hot and cold until it was just right. You would have to keep topping it up with hot to keep it warm. I would bath first, then mum. When dad came back, I had to go round to grandma's while he had his bath. If the bathtime was at night, I had to go to bed early, so that I was out of the way. Afterwards, dad had to carry the bath outside to empty it down the drain.

A coal tar shampoo ad from 1955.

Drene Shampoo – the Shampoo of the Stars – was popular for bathtime in 1946.

'The soap was nearly always Pears brand, and it was brown and transparent. My hair was washed in a shampoo called Curly Top, and it had a picture of Shirley Temple on the box. There was also a shampoo called Drene; you could cut out the top of the packet and send off for a Drene brooch, which was in the shape of a feather.

'Later on a new fire grate was put in. This had a back boiler so there was hot water most of the time for washing up and for baths, but the copper still had to be used for washing the clothes. I can remember thinking how many clothes had been washed in it when at Christmas time, it was scrubbed out and used for cooking the puddings in. Grandpa made a wooden rack so that they could be put in a double layer to cook for three or four hours. If a neighbour only made one or two Christmas puddings, they would bring them round to be cooked with ours. Despite being cooked in the boiler used for washing clothes, they still tasted wonderful.

'Even when I got married in 1954, there was no means of heating up water in the cottage we bought, except for an electric wash boiler. There wasn't a bathroom. We had a small tin bath which we used every day, but once a week we would borrow a big tin bath from my in-laws down the street. My husband had to carry it up the road on his back. I would be cross with him because as he carried the bath he used to sing. It echoed, and I said that the neighbours would think we only had a bath once a week!'

Frank Bingley remembers life in Home Farm, Gumley, and points out that the phrase 'the tin bath' is not strictly correct. 'The kitchen had a stone sink with a wooden drainer. There were no taps, so we had to fetch the water from the pump outside! Next to the sink was a brick copper with a wooden lid, though I never saw the fire lit in this, as we always boiled water up in a huge black kettle on the electric cooker. Also, with no running water available, there was no bathroom so we had to place the so-called tin bath (actually not tin but galvanised metal) in the kitchen and fill it with several kettles of water.'

Frank Bingley's brother Jeff finds a new use for the tin bath in 1959. (Frank Bingley)

You too could look as lovely as Deanna Durbin (1946).

My cousin Ann lived in a terraced house in Norman Street, Melton Mowbray, and her family had a bath in the scullery. It was boxed in most of the time, but on Friday night, the lid would come off and the whole family would have a bath. Ann's younger brother Stephen would go first, then Ann, followed by her mum and finally her dad. It was hard luck on him as everyone bathed in the same water! As in my family, the water was heated up in the big copper prior to being ladled into the actual bath. Next door to Ann lived Grandma Wainer, who had no bathroom at all, so all-over washes took place in the scullery. Moreover, Gran would not let her landlord put in electricity, as she considered it unsafe. Everything in that house, including the lights, was powered by gas. The whole house smelled of gas, but to her, that was still much safer than electricity. This continued right through the Fifties and early Sixties, and electricity was only installed in the 1960s after her death. I would guess that by then it was the only house in Melton without electricity.

Joan is so *full* of fun

Always getting up to something. So high spirited too. Taxes all your energy to keep pace with her. But in your heart you know her health is all that matters. Like all wise mothers you agree that when needed, a dose of 'California Syrup of Figs' will soon correct stomach upsets and regulate the system. It is the natural treatment for children—the laxative they like. 'California Syrup of Figs' keeps them well and happy.

"California Syrup of Figs"

Clean inside as well as out (1945)!

In my own home, we didn't actually have to use the tin bath in front of the fire, as we had a bathroom. However, on cold winter nights, we chose to use it. On Friday nights we children would have our weekly scrub in the traditional way – in the tin bath in front of the living room fire. During the rest of the year we would use the upstairs bathroom, though in summer, this would present a new problem. The water was heated by the coalfire in the living room and in hot weather, this was not lit, of course. This meant that the water for baths had to be heated in the boiler in the kitchen, whose main use was to boil the washing every Monday. Then my dad had to carry this boiling water upstairs to the bathroom in buckets, to be poured into the bath!

Kay Moon who grew up in the Spinney Hill area of Leicester says that her family had another way of getting the water from the copper to the bath. 'At bath time my mother filled the brick-built boiler and heated the water. There

43

was some sort of vacuum pump which had to be hand operated to force the water to rise into the bath upstairs. The main thing was to remember to put the plug into the bath first!'

The copper in the kitchen was not only used for heating the bath water. Jean Philps remembers, 'Although we had a bathroom with a large geyser to supply hot water, most of our baths were taken in the big brick copper situated just inside the back door. Mum would sit us on the edge to get a good soaping, then we'd go into the copper. It had a curved bottom – very dodgy if the water got too soapy.'

Finally Delia Bennett from Shepshed, who puts her memories into verse, recalls the Friday evening baths of her childhood. The final lines of her poem remind us that – for mum and dad, at least – there may have been some fun involved when taking a bath by the living room fire!

> *I recall when I was little, not much more than three or four,*
> *We used to have a tin bath which hung on our shed door,*
> *And every Friday evening, whether I was mucky or not,*
> *That tin bath was brought inside and put down on the spot*
> *Against a blazing coal fire, on a colourful old pegged rug,*
> *Then mum and dad would fill up the bath with a chipped enamel jug.*
> *After quite a lot of coaxing I'd sit down in the tub,*
> *And squirm and squeal, 'Not so hard!' as mum began to scrub.*
> *After a good going over with carbolic soap, and with skin all tingly and red,*
> *I'd quickly get dried in front of the fire, have my cocoa and go straight to bed.*
> *I never went straight to sleep though, I used to listen to mum and dad laugh;*
> *They seem to have more fun than I did, by the fireside in the old tin bath!!*

CHAPTER SIX
FISH-EYES-AND-GLUE AND THE NIT NURSE

Almost everyone who wrote to me with information for this book included some reminiscences of their schooldays, especially their days at primary school. There was so much material that a whole book could be written on this one topic. Most people had very happy memories of school though there were some less nostalgic than others.

Margaret Sparrow recalls two visitors to her school who were not altogether welcome: these were the school dentist and the nit nurse. She writes: 'I was seven years old the first time I saw the dentist on his annual school visit. He came once to examine our teeth, then a second time to give any treatment. I took a letter home for my parents to sign to agree to the treatment I needed. I was to have a tooth taken out, a big one at the back. Having a tooth pulled or filled by the school dentist was very frightening but there was no way I could get out of it. The dentist's chair was set up in front of a window in the cold, draughty porch next to the girls' cloakroom. It was white with a black step. At the side was the drill that the dentist had to operate with his foot by pedalling as fast as he could. It looked like a large bicycle wheel with a belt to drive it. It only went as fast as the dentist could pedal. When my turn came, I was given an injection to numb my gum, and then I was sent to sit on a very uncomfortable mat on the cold cloakroom floor until it was my turn again. After my tooth was taken out I was sent back to sit on the mat again with a large piece of cotton wool in my mouth until it had stopped bleeding. I can remember walking home from school that day feeling very sorry for myself.

'Twice a year we would get a visit from the nit nurse. She used to arrive in the morning and spend most of the day at school. We had to stand in a line so that she could look in our hair to see if we had nits or head lice. This was awful because she found some in mine. I had to have some dreadful smelling oil which my mother got from the chemist, put on my head. Every night I had to comb my hair with a fine-tooth comb over some paper to get out the dead nits. Sometimes there were still some live ones, and you had to kill them by crushing them with your thumbnail. I had to sit at a desk on my own in the classroom so that I didn't pass them on to someone else. Everyone knew why I was sitting on my own and I felt so ashamed. The evacuees were blamed for the problem; everyone said they had brought the nits with them.'

Jean Philps is one person who thought her early days of school were wonderful. Writing of her first class at Sharnford school, she says, 'My first

Pupils at Stanton-under-Bardon school 1942-3.
(Margaret Sparrow)

A wartime party
at Stanton school.
(Margaret Sparrow)

St Mary's infants' school in Norman Street, Melton.
(Arnold Jordan)

teacher was Miss Rose Metcalf, who was the daughter of the rector of Frolesworth. She had the most loving and gentle nature, and we all adored her. She was our second mother. Mid-morning, we all had a little bottle of milk with a straw. Most of us took a piece of fruit to school, usually an orange, and the smell of oranges always reminds me of those early schooldays. We wrote on slates and formed our first letters and numbers with chalk and charcoal sticks. By the 1950s, I had now progressed from Miss Metcalf's class to Mr Pratt's in the larger schoolroom. He was a strict disciplinarian and his cane was kept in the stock cupboard at the back of his desk. It only came out when absolutely necessary – we generally behaved!'

Not all schools waited for absolute necessity before bringing out the cane. I once nearly got the cane at the age of six, simply for joining the end of a queue without checking the front of it! I was at St Mary's infants' school in Norman Street, Melton Mowbray where the headmistress was Miss Sibley. She was very strict, although I always got on well with her. This stood me in good stead on one occasion when, one lunchtime, I noticed a queue of seven-year-old boys leading into school. I rather fancied being inside and joined the end. As we got into school, the head of the queue led into Miss Sibley's classroom. The boys went into the room one by one, and to my horror, I realised that each boy was being caned. I was too petrified to escape back into the yard and when it came to my turn, I went up to her desk. She looked at me and said, 'Surely you haven't been running up the coke pile, David!' 'No, Miss Sibley,' I replied, and to my relief, was ordered back out into the yard. I learned an important lesson from this: never join the end of a queue without checking to see what it's leading to. My only excuse must be that this was wartime, and people were usually queuing because some item in short supply had appeared in a shop. If you spotted a queue, joining it was the normal reaction.

Some correspondents regretted the disappearance of the cane as an instrument of discipline. One such is Margaret Johnson who went to a school in a suburb of Leicester in the mid-1960s. 'In my primary school there didn't seem to be much discipline. We were in mixed ability classes and some of the rougher and naughtier children seemed to get away with anything. I think a touch of the stick would have done wonders for them. The years before the Sixties were much better for law and order in the classroom.'

Anne Silins might disagree. Recalling her school in Appleby Magna in the

The author in Melton Mowbray boys' primary school uniform.

1940s, she says, 'Rules were strict, and when not working with our hands, we were expected to sit upright with them folded in our lap. The teacher paraded the room with a wooden cane at the ready. "If I see one hand fidgeting, it's the cane," she would warn. One day my skirt had bunched up under my bottom and as I had been told by my grandma to keep my knees covered, I reached down to set it straight. My unlucky day. Whack! There was a long red mark across the back of my hand, which developed into a red blister by home time. I had learned my lesson: from now on showing a bit of knee was the least of my worries. I had felt the sting of the cane so I would just be unladylike.'

The cane wasn't the only form of punishment that might seem barbaric in retrospect. Anne Silins again. 'After a year at the Church School I was moved to the Girls' School in North Street, Ashby-de-la-Zouch. I was a very nervous, fidgety, couldn't-sit-still little girl, who bit her nails and always had a frown on her face. I must have been more nervous than usual on one particular day.

Outdoor PT at Melton boys' primary school 1947-8.

Whatever the reason, the teacher locked me in her cloakroom as a punishment. The door closed and was locked from the outside. I turned to confront the darkness. Dry-mouthed, terrified and longing to protest my innocence, I inched along the wall, hitting my head on empty coat hooks. Only the yellow ribbon of light outlining the door was clear. I was positive there were monsters, all sorts of creatures in the dark.

'I was in that cloakroom the entire afternoon. At the end of the day, the teacher let me out. I was curled up in a corner, almost incoherent. She must have been alarmed because she took me to get my coat and bag, then walked me to the school gates. I fled down the alleyway to Market Street and the bus stop, not knowing if I was early or late. My black knickers were damp and my uniform stained; my weak bladder had let me down again. When I arrived home, grandma did not ask questions, she just took my knickers and threw them on the back of the fire. My pride was hurt, and grandma sat close to me as we shared tea. Her sister-in-law sometimes did supply teaching at my new school, and a message was sent that the family thought my punishment had been very unfair. After a while my teacher became a little kinder to me and I soon found that I enjoyed my new school.'

One piece of school architecture mentioned by several Leicestershire residents was the school stove to be found in each classroom. Jean Philps writes, 'The classroom was heated by a big black stove surrounded by a high guard. How glad our teacher must have been to warm herself after cycling from Frolesworth on a cold winter morning.' Anne Silins remembers another use of the stove: 'There was a big iron stove in each room, set up against the wall, surrounded by a guard to stop us from falling against it. It also served as a place to hang wet coats, scarfs and hats on rainy days. Boots – after being cleaned off at the boot scraper outside the door – were placed around the guard, their open ends towards the heat, fanning out like the spokes of an enormous wheel. It came as a complete surprise to me that some children's boots had holes or even great rips in their soles. Water from wading in puddles or in the brook went into these boots, so when they came off in the cloakroom, water spilt out making the floor one enormous puddle. Of course, none of our clothing dried out by dinner time, so we slopped home and repeated the whole procedure in the afternoon.'

In the latter school, all the children obviously went home for their mid-day dinner. In the towns, we stayed for school dinners. As far as I remember, these

Form 1-0 at Melton Grammar School in 1950.

were perfectly edible, although we routinely grumbled about them, giving the various meals deliberately revolting names, *frogspawn* or *snot pie* for example. I had a healthy appetite and ate anything they put in front of me, which is perhaps as well since my mum was one of the dinner ladies. Jean Philps remembers her school meals at Mount Grace High School in Hinckley which she describes as wonderful, adding, 'I've never tasted custard as creamy, or had such delicious beef pie. And the trifles were to die for!'

Anne Silins' memories of her school dinners in her Ashby school are less pleasant: 'When the bell rang at noon, we all trooped into the big echoing room and took our places at the tables, each set for twelve students. Each table had a senior prefect at the end closest to the kitchen. As we said the usual "for-what-we-are-about-to-receive" we all looked down at our plates. They were filled with over-cooked potatoes, boiled meat and brussels sprouts which had been boiled for at least seventeen hours. I was never a good eater, so I picked away until it was time for the pudding. "No pudding if you don't finish the first course!" the servers yelled. I hardly ever got to eat pudding, but I didn't mind, especially if it was tapioca. We called tapioca *fish-eyes-and-glue*, which is exactly what it looked like.

'My Mum the Dinner Lady' and her colleagues in 1948 (left to right back: Con Ruddle, Olive Ruddle; front: Doris Pearce, Carol Southgate, Joan Bell and Mrs Bannister).

'When I told my uncle about the food, he had a suggestion. Under the trestle table we used at school, there would be a small shelf right below the main bracing. Why didn't I put my greens or other bits I couldn't eat on this little shelf? He assured me that no one would know who'd done it, and that way I could get my pudding! I would have to remember to change my seat regularly, so that the bits of food didn't always fall from the same spot when the tables were put away after dinner.

'The tactic worked for several weeks, but the prefects and servers had met this ploy before. I was caught out. Wouldn't you just know that the day I was caught out, the meal was boiled meat and sprouts. I was told to sit until I had finished the whole plate, then if I was lucky, I could have my pudding. I sat and stared at my plate for what seemed like hours. I sat swinging my feet, and watched as the whole dining room and kitchen were cleaned. Finally, towards three o'clock, the staff got fed up with me as they wanted to go home. They all stood round me as I stuffed the cold food covered in congealed fat into my mouth, groaning and retching the whole time. "Now," they announced, "I could have my pudding." It was awful – cold steamed pudding covered in cold custard! It hit my stomach like a piece of stone and I started to cry. This worked I should have tried it much sooner. I suspect the women all wanted to go. "Go home," they said. By now it was time to run for the bus and I did.'

CHAPTER SEVEN
THE VILLAGE SHOP AND THE CO-OP

Jean Philps recalls the days when her village of Sharnford had lots of shops. She writes, 'Apart from our family's butcher shop, there was the post office and grocery stores. Next door – up two great steps – was Harry Cooper's paper shop. This business was conducted from his front room, which would be full of newspapers, plus buckets of fresh flowers and piles of vegetables

The Cosy Cafe, Sharnford in the 1950s.
(Jean Philps)

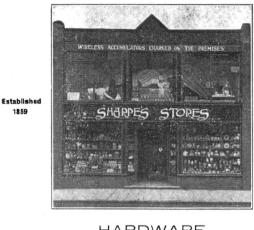

Established 1859

Phone 96

WIRELESS ACCUMULATORS CHARGED ON THE PREMISES

SHARPES STORES

HARDWARE
GLASS   CHINA
AND
EARTHENWARE

PAINT   DISTEMPER
WALLPAPER

ALL HOUSEHOLD BRUSHES

*WE ALSO COVER A WIDE COUNTRY AREA
WITH OUR MOBILE SHOP*

Sharpes Stores were one of many that kept villagers supplied via their mobile shop.

SHARPES STORES

(MELTON) LTD.

NOTTINGHAM STREET   MELTON MOWBRAY

from his allotment. At the bottom of the hill by the bridge stood a garage and a fish and chip shop, which was originally a wooden building but it was replaced by a brick building when it burnt down. In School Lane was a little shop selling groceries and best of all sweets – very popular for pupils at the nearby school. The Cosy Café – now called the Sharnford House Restaurant – had an Aladdin's cave at one end of the building selling curios and antiques. At Christmas toys appeared amid hundreds of fairy lights. It was a thrill to press your nose to the window and look in. Once a fortnight, Mr Swinfin's travelling shop swung and swayed up the lane laden with pots, pans, brushes and mops hanging on hooks around the outside of the van.' She adds that, sadly, only the post office and garage now remain.

Frank Bingley of Gumley, a much smaller village in the south west of the county recalls how his community was served by travelling shops. 'There were several traders who regularly came to our village. Herbert came every Saturday and the sides of his lorry would open up to form a canopy when it rained. It was crammed full of goodies, including fruit, vegetables, chocolate, sweets, cans of food, everything. I would spend my pocket money there every week, and have something nice to eat while watching *Take Your Pick* with Michael Miles on the TV. Jack would come round with his little van selling bakery foods on certain days. Penny cobs were deliciously fresh and crusty. He also sold chocolate, especially Penguins and Caramel Bars.

'Other people that came regularly included Patsy Garton in his pony and trap; he would always take the children for rides up and down the village. A little old lady called Mary Cryer also came through the village on a regular basis. She came from Foxton and she would walk from village to village. Goodness knows how far she walked in a day! My friends and I didn't use to speak to her though, as she had a severe speech impediment and we could never make out what she said! The milkman was as regular as clockwork. I used to love the little bottles of fresh orange juice that he carried. When my mother paid him, she didn't pay with money, but with little square shiny silver coloured tokens with Co-operative Society stamped on them.'

Recalling Shepshed in the 1960s, Judith Thompson recalls the oddities of Sunday shopping when some items were available but others were not able to be legally sold.

'There was a corner shop on Belton Street, where Nana and Grandpa Bowler lived, and this opened on Sunday mornings. They could not sell shampoo, but Grandpa would send me for 10 Woodbines, 3d worth of Extra Strong Mints and a 7 o'clock razor blade. I would also take Grandpa's empty beer bottles back to the Blue Bell pub for the 1d refund.'

The shop I remember best from my childhood in Melton Mowbray was the corner shop that stood where Elmhurst Avenue joined Welby Lane. It was run by Cyril Everley, a former Derbyshire miner, and it sold groceries, fruit and veg, cigarettes, sweets, and anything else that local people might need. Cyril was quite a character and, as children, we were very impressed that every sentence he uttered contained at least five swear words. We didn't know any other adults that swore, so this man was unique. Actually he only ever used two different swear words, *bloody* and *bugger* (which he pronounced *bogger*), both of which would seem very mild today. We enjoyed quoting Cyril verbatim although our parents didn't encourage this practice.

When I was in my teens, I worked there on Saturdays and after school on weekdays, a job my younger sister Joan later took on. Working at the shop was quite an eye-opener. Some customers would try to get goods on credit ('on tick'), but I had to clear this with Cyril as he knew who were the bad payers. Some of the customers had difficulty with their words and malapropisms were quite common. Several used to ask for 'a quarter of Typhoon tea' but they were not as bad as the elderly lady who always wanted 'Typhoid tea'! All the

Stalls in Melton's Sherrard Street, 1950
(Arnold Jordan)

tea was in the form of leaves of course, as the days of tea bags were still in the distant future. All the sweets were kept in large jars and had to be weighed out into paper bags, usually in 4oz or 2oz quantities. Anyone asking for ½lb of sweets (8oz) was regarded as having more money than sense, and being a spendthrift. Cigarettes were sold to anyone, though we sometimes asked children, 'Are they for your dad?' knowing all the time that they weren't.

Another memorable shop in Melton was the Co-op. The best thing here was the wonderful system of obtaining change. There were no tills at the counters, so if you paid with a ten shilling note, this was put with details of your purchase into a metal cylinder, and sent by overhead wire to the cashier who worked in an office high up on one wall. She would put in your change and send it back down to the shop assistants. Three of the overhead wires ran to counters in the shop, but others ran through holes in the wall to the Co-op butcher and cobbler next door! The cylinders were sent up to the cashier by a spring mechanism, but came back by means of gravity.

The other procedure unique to the Co-op was the divi. Every customer

Cheapside in Melton, decorated for the Coronation in 1953.
(Arnold Jordan)

received a dividend back once a year, based on how much they had spent. This meant that every time you went in and bought something, you had to quote your individual divi number. My mum's divi number – 4306 – is permanently etched on my memory (and I am someone who cannot normally remember numbers). My grandmother's number was even more memorable. She was a very early member of the Co-op and her divi number was 60. One thing that the Co-op had in common with the corner shop was that you could send in an order to be delivered to your house the same day. You then paid for it when you took in your next week's order. Home deliveries – now being promoted by modern supermarkets as a wonderful new idea – were what most of us took for granted in the 50s.

Milk was delivered to your house by a milkman, but if you had it from the Co-op, you actually paid for it with plastic tokens bought from the main grocery shop (or delivered with your order). Each token bought one pint of milk, so that the milkman never had to bother with change. If you left out two milk tokens you got two pints of milk. Our tokens were always blue because we had pasteurised milk, though there were also green tokens for those who preferred sterilised milk. I couldn't understand why anyone would drink sterilised milk as it tasted awful. I think perhaps it kept longer than the pasteurised variety. As we had no fridges then, it was necessary to stand the milk bottles in a bucket of cold water in summer. It still used to get a bit sour in very hot weather, though, and there would be little blobs of it floating in your tea. We also had bread delivered, but that came in a little brown van belonging to Beaver's the bakers who had a shop on the corner of Nottingham Street and Norman Street, next to Woods the petshop.

Of course, there was one main item of shopping that interested us. With our pocket money in the 40s and 50s we bought sweets, and the one that I remember the most vividly was called Kali (pronounced *Kay-lie*). This was a yellow crystally powder, and we bought it in 2oz cone-shaped paper bags. To eat Kali, we sucked our finger then dipped it in the powder. The Kali stuck to the wet finger and when you sucked it again, the Kali fizzed and exploded on your tongue. It was wonderful. More sophisticated children bought a liquorice tube with their Kali, and they sucked it through that, but in our part of town it was always the wet finger method.

My cousin Ann says that she used to make a drink by adding water to Kali, and that it also came in a red version, but to me Kali was always yellow, and the idea of diluting its fizzy taste with water sounds like sacrilege. Ann also remembers her childhood sweets and lists her favourites as sherbet fountains, liquorice shoelaces, gob stoppers, lucky bags, ½d chews, spangles and liquorice comfits ('especially the red ones which could be used as lipstick!'). Ann seems to have had access to more sweets than me but, being nine years younger, her childhood and teenage years would have been in the 50s and 60s. I'm sure she can't remember sweets being on ration. I can; I remember feeling very grown-up when my mum gave me my sweet coupons to buy my own sweets when I was 10 or 11.

Today, most of the village shops have gone, and even in the towns many of the individual shops have either disappeared or are in danger of doing so. They have been driven out by competition from the large out-of-town supermarkets, where they can often sell things cheaper. I am not unrealistic,

Melton Co-op. (Derek Whitehouse)

and I realise that even those people who complain about the disappearance of the small shops probably get their own groceries from the supermarket. However, in common with many other Leicestershire residents, I do look back with nostalgia to the days when every town and village had its own wide range of individual shops.

CHAPTER EIGHT
GOING TO THE PICTURES

Mary Yendall says that in the postwar days of the 1940s, 'our number one amusement seemed to be the cinema. The Futurist was the name of the one in Sileby, but to us it was always known as *Bert's Bug House*. Here, for the princely sum of 3d, we could watch two main films, the Pathé news, and a serial which would have us on the edge of our seat. The evening always ended with the playing of the national anthem, for which we had to stand to attention until the last chord was played. Homeward bound, we would call at Cal's fish and chip shop and ask for three-pennyworth of chips and plenty of scratchings (the bits of batter which had fallen off the fish). This truly gourmet feast was wrapped in newspaper, with lashings of salt and vinegar, and it always tasted better when eaten al fresco.'

By tradition, the cinema was useful for more than watching films. It was one of the few

The Regal and the Plaza operated an odd system, showing the same films in rotation.

REGAL: MELTON MOWBRAY

Manager: A. Scarborough   Phone 2251

SUNDAY, OCTOBER 6th   FOR ONE DAY

5.40 **MONEY, WOMEN. AND GUNS** (U) 8.45
JOCK MAHONEY   KIM HUNTER
Also Jack Hawkins in THE PLANTER'S WIFE (A) 7.15

MONDAY, OCTOBER 7th   FOR THREE DAYS
THE LIST OF ADRIAN MESSENGER
5.35 8.35 (A)
TONY CURTIS   KIRK DOUGLAS
Also Audie Murphy & Kathleen Crowley in SHOWDOWN (A) 7.15

THURSDAY, OCTOBER 10th   FOR THREE DAYS
7.15 **THE COURTSHIP OF EDDIE'S FATHER** (U)
GLENN FORD   SHIRLEY JONES
Also Connie Francis in FOLLOW THE BOYS (U) 5.35 9.10

Bingo at The Plaza

TUESDAY, FRIDAY and SATURDAY
Doors Open 6.45 p.m. for 8 p.m. prompt
GOLDEN SCOOP EACH EVENING
PAID OUT LAST WEEK: £369.13.6

By the 1960s the Plaza had become a bingo hall.

indoor places where you could be alone with your current sweetheart. Anne Jones from Kirby Muxloe tells me that in the 1950s the village of Ratby had its own cinema with double seats on the back row designed for courting couples. We had nothing like that in Melton; we had to manage with the arms of the seat as a barrier between us! Anne also remembers Leicester's cinemas: the art deco style Odeon, the Picture House, the Gaumont, the Savoy, the Cameo, the Princes, plus the inevitable fleapit (the Floral Hall). These were all in the city centre, but further out in the suburbs there were the Shaftesbury, the Roxy, the Regal, the Olympia and the Trocadero.

Anne's mention of the Floral Hall reminds me that when I was 13 or 14, I used to go on the train to Leicester with a couple of friends on a Saturday afternoon. We would often go to the pictures and our favourite venue was the seedy little Floral Hall cinema, which specialised in X-rated foreign films with subtitles. Of course, there was some dross, but I remember seeing some great pictures there, including *The Wages of Fear* and *Les Diaboliques*, now regarded as classics.

We didn't need to go to Leicester however. Melton boasted two cinemas in the Fifties, the Regal and the Plaza. These stood next to each other in King Street, and were owned by the same family, the Scarboroughs. A film would be shown at the Regal on Monday, Tuesday and Wednesday, then transfer to the Plaza for the rest of the week. The film, which began the week at the Plaza, would be shown at the Regal afterwards. This seemed perfectly normal at the time, but slightly odd in retrospect. On Sundays a different film was shown; this was often an X film, possibly on the grounds that if you were wicked enough to go to the pictures on a Sunday, you would probably appreciate a violent or sexy adult film! The 750 seat Plaza was the older of the two cinemas, having opened as the Picture House in 1920. It lasted as a cinema until 1962 when it became a bingo hall, and was finally demolished in 1974 to make room for a road. Its larger neighbour, the Regal opened in 1933 and, surprisingly in these days of multi-screen cinemas, is still showing films today.

While there were people who liked the older and cosier Plaza, we youngsters preferred the bigger brasher Regal because it had an upstairs. The seats up in

The Regal cinema in the 1950s. (Pauline Black)

◆ **'LET'S GO TO THE PICTURES'** ◆

THE A.L.A. MOBILE

CINEMA

EVERY WEEK at 7.30 in the VILLAGE HALL

DUNTON BASSETT	**WELFORD**	**CLAYBROOKE**
ON MONDAYS	ON TUESDAYS	ON WEDNESDAYS

PAILTON ON THURSDAYS — **WOLVEY** ON FRIDAYS

Presenting THE BEST in screen entertainment . . . . .
plus events of the day in GAUMONT BRITISH NEWS

Let us send you our MONTHLY PROGRAMME

PRIVATE SHOWS can be arranged with the latest
SOUND EQUIPMENT at anytime, and anywhere

For full information please write to :—
44 MARKET STREET, LUTTERWORTH

Mobile cinemas would put on shows in the local village hall – this ad from 1952.

the balcony cost 1/9, compared with 9d for the cheapest seats downstairs. My dad could never understand why we would pay a shilling more but for us the balcony was the only place to be seen. If you went with a group of mates, all male, then you would sit at the front of the balcony smoking cigarettes, but if you were taking a young lady then the only possible seats were on the balcony's back row. There you could watch the occasional bit of the film, but spend most of your time snogging, interrupted occasionally by the beam of torchlight shone by the inquisitive usherette, whose job involved showing the patrons to their seats, but also keeping her eye on the back row activities.

The other special showing at the Regal was the Saturday afternoon children's special, when you could see at least two films plus a serial. The one I remember best was the adventures of Flash Gordon, who travelled through space to fight evil aliens like Emperor Ming. Each episode would end with Flash in some terrible predicament where he looked bound to die, but at the beginning of next week's episode he would manage to escape. I gradually worked out that the makers of the serial actually cheated, after one episode ended with our hero falling right down into a fiery furnace, whereas the beginning of the next week's show began with him falling only part way in, and surviving to climb out unscathed. I think the seeds of my distrust of authority in general may have been sowed at this point.

Films at this time were divided into U films, A films and X films. The first category was suitable for both children and adults, the A films were for accompanied children, while X films were restricted to over 16s. However, the cinema staff didn't enforce these rules at all to begin with. I remember going to see *The Beast With Five Fingers* with my mate Maurice when we were 9 or 10. When the severed hand of the title began to creep upstairs to murder someone, Maurice (destined later to become a fearless burly policeman) began to howl with terror, which led to both of us being evicted from the cinema.

People from the villages used to catch a bus into town to go to the pictures, but some of the more remote places had a travelling cinema which would show films in their village hall. Jean Philps recalled that 'on Monday nights the travelling cinema came to Sharnford, and we sat on benches at the front and cheered our heroes Hopalong Cassidy, Gene Autry and Buck Jones. The first colour picture we saw was *State Fair* starring Jeanne Crain and Dana Andrews. We also saw Bela Lugosi as Dracula, which stuck in my mind for weeks afterwards. The old stove smoked, the draughts through the windows were terrible and when the rain beat on the tin roof, we could hardly hear the film, but we were not put off.' The films children watched obviously influenced their games, and Jean continues, 'Grandad had a butcher's shop and there were plenty of outbuildings. In one of the large garages was an old converted meat wagon, which was ideal when we played our favourite game – cowboys and indians. My brothers had silver replicas of the handguns seen in the films, and guess who had the feathers in her hair! Feathers were easy to come by, as the orchard had all kinds of poultry scratching there.'

Jean's comments bring back the memory of how we used to leave the cinema when we were children. When we had watched a film, we would walk down the steps of the Regal with our heads still buzzing with what we'd seen. If it had been a cops-and-robbers film we would be on the lookout for gangsters behaving suspiciously, but if it had been a western, most of us would swagger out of the Regal with our hand itching to draw our pistols on any baddies. We would be sure to recognise them as they would be the ones wearing black hats. Life was much simpler then, when the heroes were the ones wearing white hats and the villains wore black!

CHAPTER NINE

BIKES, BUSES AND A YELLOW ROLLS-ROYCE

I n the late 1940s, there was only one car in our street. If we saw it being backed out of its drive, my friend and I would beg its owner for a ride. He would give us a lift as far as the corner shop, and we would walk back bragging, 'We've been in a car!' to anyone we saw. Cars were not as speedy as today and our top compliment if we saw a really big car was, 'I bet that'll do sixty!'

Not everyone grew up as car-less as I did. Grizelda Hargreaves of Market Bosworth grew up with a very special family car. Her father – Richard Derrington Fenning – managed the Royal Hotel in Ashby-de-la-Zouch, and his car was a yellow Rolls-Royce. It was used for normal family outings and even – somewhat to Grizelda's embarrassment – for running her to school. Once a year it found local fame when it led the Life Boat Fund

Richard Derrington Fenning and his yellow Rolls-Royce.

Barton's Buses ran local routes, and also provided coaches to meet the growing demand for holiday travel.

parade through Ashby. After Grizelda's family had parted with the Rolls, it found even more fame as the car used in *The Darling Buds of May* television series.

Jean Philps' family also owned cars, and she remembers making an annual family journey by car from Sharnford to Great Yarmouth in the late Forties and early Fifties. 'We would set off at the crack of dawn in the little Ford, with my Aunt Min and Uncle Orm. Our breakfast of bacon and egg was eaten on the roadside near some woods along the way. It took most of the day to get there but it was worth it. I also recall going to Leicester with Grandad Orton and Uncle Orm in the Buick, which smelled of leather and cigars. They would park at the top of the market, and I would stay in the back seat of the car with an ice-cream while Grandad and Uncle met friends in the Jetty Wine Shop.

'Uncle Orm worked for Brindleys Transport, and often I would go with him in his lorry, which had the engine in the middle of the cab. It was incredibly noisy, but we would sing at the top of our voices as we went along. His load consisted of great concrete arches which were delivered to Corby – probably to construct the great chimneys of the steelworks there. Another gentler mode of transport was Dolly the mare. Uncle Tom (grandad's unmarried brother who lived with him) was in charge of the pony and trap. The poor horse didn't know where she was as Uncle Tom told her to "Gee-up" and in the next breath to "Whoa-back." Still it was great to travel the country lanes to the clip-clop of Dolly's hooves.'

In my own childhood, most of our transport was on the bus or on Shanks's Pony (i.e. on foot). The buses in Melton were all Barton's, and one of them went into town from the corner of our street every quarter of an hour. It cost 1d (old penny) for an adult to go the 1½ miles into town, half price for children of course. Barton's Buses were a maroon colour, and for a while I firmly believed all buses were this colour. Then I discovered that the Midland Red buses that ran between Leicester and Grantham were a different shade of red. It was a great shock when on one occasion the Midland Red bus was replaced by a Lincoln Green one. A green bus? The world was obviously a bigger and more varied place then I had supposed! Of course all buses had a driver and a conductor. The latter would collect your 1d fare as the bus was going along; there was no question of the driver bothering with mundane matters like money. His job was to concentrate on the driving.

We walked about a mile and a half to school in the morning, along with a group of older children, who would often let us accompany them into the grounds of Stavely Lodge where there was a huge conker tree and a fascinating underground air-raid shelter to be explored. We never mentioned this detour to our parents, though. We always caught the bus home from school just after 4 o'clock. In 1950, when I was 11, I had my first bike, a

The author's first bike, 1950.

Hercules. I was very proud of it for a year or two, then began to nag for a more grown-up bike with dropped handlebars. I used to cycle to the grammar school as it was about three miles. We would bike through the town, swoop down from the railway bridge round a double bend and then up Burton Hill. I remember one frosty morning, when the roads were icy in places, a girl called Bernice Parr fell off her bike as we approached the bottom of Burton Hill. As I zoomed past her sitting on the road, I turned to laugh at her. Whatever gods disapprove of such lack of gallantry whipped my bike from beneath me and left me sliding on my back along the road. There is such a thing as rough justice.

There was a strictly enforced school rule about cycling home. We had to dismount at the top of the hill and push our cycles down to the bottom. No one was exempt from this, except for one wonderfully eccentric teacher called Miss Howarth who used to zoom past us on her large sit-up-and-beg bike with her feet up in the air. As I trudged along pushing my bike, I used to watch with envy.

When my sister had a bike, I persuaded her to come on a weekend trip to the YHA youth hostel called Shining Cliff near Ambergate in Derbyshire. We biked the 50 miles there on a Saturday, stayed at the hostel overnight, then came home on the Sunday. This was somewhat thoughtless of me, as Joan had only had her bike for a fortnight and had never been more than fives miles on it! A typical big brother really.

In the late 1950s I swapped my bike for a motor scooter. There were only two makes in those days, Lambrettas and Vespas. The Vespa had rounded 'hips'

The author on his Vespa, 1959.

Cars were beginning to be seen on the roads in more numbers by 1949 when this ad appeared.

whereas the Lambretta was built on straighter lines. I decided on a Vespa, partly because that was what Len Manchester's garage sold, and our next-door neighbour, Frank Tyler, was a director there. Another reason for the

The author's first car,
a Morris Minor,
with his sister Joan
at the wheel.

choice was that the Vespa came in a 125cc and 150cc version. I went for the more powerful one. I bought the Vespa on a Saturday morning, had a ten-minute lesson on Melton's old aerodrome from the garage mechanic, then rode it around the town for half an hour in the afternoon. The next day I rode it back to college, some 60 miles away. Rather foolish perhaps, but we were more relaxed about such things in those days.

One thing I remember from riding a scooter in the 1950s is that if you had mechanical trouble and pulled into a lay-by, within minutes another motorcyclist or scooter rider would pull in beside you with a cheerful, 'Got a problem, mate?' The *mods v rockers* nonsense, which divided scooter fans from motorbike enthusiasts was still a decade away.

It was the mid-1960s before I moved on to my first car. I bought this car, a Morris Minor with a canvas hood and a split windscreen, from my sister since – despite being four years younger than me – she had learned to drive first. This vehicle would now be a collector's item and worth a small fortune, but I think when I traded it in for a Morris Traveller a few years later the garage allowed me £6 for it!

Frank Bingley did his learning to drive in the Fifties, while he was still a child. He grew up in the village of Gumley, near Market Harborough, and like many a member of a farming community, he learned on the family tractor. 'Sometimes, even at an early age, I was allowed to drive the tractor while my stepfather threw the portions of hay off the trailer. One day, I was running out of the field, and there was a gate just ahead. The trouble was, there was a steep bank down to the gate, and the field was muddy. My stepfather shouted, "Put yer foot on the brake!" Being rather small at that age, I got the thing out of gear, but couldn't reach the brake from the seat. I jumped off the seat and onto one of the two brake pedals. As I had all my weight on one pedal, one wheel locked, and I just slide on the mud straight through the gate in spectacular fashion! I was not allowed to drive the tractor for some time after that.'

The 1950s David Brown tractor which Frank crashed through the gate, here driven by his stepfather.
(Frank Bingley)

Melton's Northern Station – the Gateway to Skegness! (Derek Whitehouse)

Our other form of transport was the train. Back in those good old days, Melton had two railway stations. One was the Town Station serving the LMS line to Leicester or to Peterborough, where you could change for London. The other, called the Northern Station, served the LNER line; this was the line to Skegness on the east coast, and was thus the station used when going on holiday. This station finally closed in 1964.

In the early 1950s, I collected train numbers with my schoolfriends. Actually I wasn't a purist train spotter, since I was only interested in those trains that were *namers* (ie they had a name like *The Prince of Wales* rather than just a boring number). Wherever we were in town, if we could see the signals, a cry would go up, 'Train pegged!' and we would cycle like mad to get to the station before the train came in. On one occasion, I biked so hard for 1^1/$_2$ miles that, although I got there in time, I passed out just as the train arrived. My mates were adamant that I couldn't count that *namer* in my collection as I had been flat out on the ground and therefore hadn't actually seen it. Ten years later, I used the LMS line when I began teaching in Leicester. I had to catch a bus into town at 7.15 am, then the train – a proper steam train, of course – to Leicester. The return journey on the train had one snag; I often fell asleep and had to rely on the jolt as the train stopped at Melton station to wake me up!

CHAPTER TEN
BIG NIGHTS OUT

As everyone keeps telling me, 'Back in the Forties and Fifties, we made our own entertainment.' Stella James recalls, 'Every summer holiday I would go to Barsby to stay with my grandma. While there I would go for cycle rides round the area with friends, and play dressing up. Every Christmas and Easter, my parents, my sister Rosemary and I would go to stay with my Aunt Dot and Uncle Dick at Skeffington. We ate farm food and had roaring log fires. I used to feed the chickens there, and help wash up. Upstairs was a long passage leading to the bedrooms. On wet days we would put on old socks of my uncle's and have great fun sliding up and down the polished floor. It was a cold house unless you were near a fire. At Christmas tea there would be seventeen of us. We would play card games – snap and Happy Families – and any games we'd had for Christmas.'

Mary McDonald of Sileby adds, 'Life as a child was good. There was not much traffic and plenty of open space to play our games. Playing mostly in a gang, games of skipping, whip and top, bowl a hoop, hide and seek, knock and run, cock-a-rusty, marbles, tick off ground, tag and scrumping, just for a bit of devilment. With a bottle of water and a dripping doorstep (bread cut thickly) we could roam the fields and not come to any harm. Yes, I would say that life was great.'

Jean Philps of Sharnford is another lady who recalls the outdoor days of her childhood with nostalgia. 'In the long summer holidays we would be off up the fields with bottles of cold tea and jam sandwiches. We took fishing nets made with a wire ring with a stocking foot attached, pushed into a garden cane. Often on the Fosse, there would be gypsy caravans, all beautifully carved and painted. We were scared to walk past as the gypsies sat on the grass verges with their fires burning, washing spread over the hedges and their horses grazing. They were the true Romany, and there was never a scrap of rubbish – everything was burned or buried. Sometimes our mothers would take us to the bridge on the Frolesworth Road where the brook was deep enough to swim.'

Frank Bingley makes his childhood in the south-east of the county sound idyllic. 'Gumley is set in one of the most beautiful parts of Leicestershire, surrounded by hilly fields, woods and spinneys, and when I was young, we had all these places to explore. Sometimes in summer, during the school holidays, I would get up very early and be out of the house well before six o'clock. It felt so good to ramble through the woods at that time of day, and the dawn chorus would be absolutely deafening. There were certainly a lot more birds about in those days, and the air was so fresh, it fair made you dizzy.

Sharnford Carnival Queen 1950.
(Jean Philps)

'By the side of the roads, the keck would grow tall. Its hollow stems sliced in lengths of about eight inches with a penknife would make ideal pea shooters. Little did we know then, that it was poisonous! At the back of Hall Farm there was a spinney full of hazel trees on a steep bank down to the field called Cackruff. These were full of nuts to eat in the autumn, and around each clump of trees were lots of suckers which grew long and straight. These were used as binders to twist around stakes in a newly laid hedge, but we had other uses for it. A six foot length of these hazel suckers had a very springy quality and made an excellent bow with a piece of baler twine pulled tight from end to end. Smaller pieces were used as arrows which we would slit at one end and insert a hen or pigeon feather. We would also cut elaborate patterns in the bark of the bow with a penknife which really made them look special.'

Not all entertainment was home-made. Sometimes attractions would come to your village. Jean Philps continues, 'In September, the fair would arrive amid great excitement. It meant swingboats, cockerel roundabouts, dodgems, toffee

Sharnford Silver Band 1953. (Jean Philps)

The author in a transvestite stage with his sister Joan in a fancy dress competition in 1953.

apples, candy floss, the noise and smell of the engines driving the carousels, music and all the fun of the fair. A travelling circus once visited, which was a real treat. We also had carnivals up to the early 50s. The carnival queen and her attendants would be on the back of a decorated Brindley's lorry, with people in fancy dress following in procession, all led by Sharnford Silver Band. They would do a tour round the village, then on to the cricket field for the judging of the best fancy dress. The carnival queen presented sporting trophies to the village football and cricket clubs. There would be sideshows, a tug-o-war, sports and dancing to finish off the day.'

For Mary Yendall, it was the May Day parade of the Forties that she remembers. 'When peace was declared after six long years, life began to get back to how it used to be. Once more, Sileby began to hold their spectacular May parade. Folk would travel from far afield to watch.'

Even in the 1960s, the village festivals were still being held. Judith Thompson recalls, 'Shepshed Wakes, held on the Dovecote down Butt Hole, were the highlights of the year. It seemed everyone in the village went – a real social gathering. I remember fluffy monkeys on sticks, soft plastic black dolls with gold hoop earrings, coconut shies, dodgems, toffee apples, brandy snaps, hook-a-duck, and winning goldfish in small carry-home plastic bags. On the Saturday night, we would meet Grandma Berridge at the Brit (the Britannia Inn on Field Street). She would be outside in the garden, weather permitting, drinking barley wine, with some of my great uncles who had travelled from Loughborough for the occasion. They would give me a treat – perhaps half-a-crown – or buy me an *okey* (ice-cream) from the Okey Pokey man. Strawberry Cream soda was my drink of the day, or Dandelion and Burdock, with a packet of crisps including salt in a little blue bag.'

As children turned into teenagers, other forms of entertainment held sway, including the dance hall. Kay Moon of Leicester has one great memory of her

A teenage Kay Moon. (Kay Moon)

Dressing up for the Saturday night dance in 1955.

dancing days. 'I used to enjoy going to dances with my friend Anne. On one occasion we were at the Palais de Danse when we were approached by a very presentable young man. He said to me, "My friend over there wants to dance with you." I looked *over there* and saw that the friend was a very tall, very dark, handsome young man in a light coloured suit. "Why doesn't he come and ask me himself?" I asked. "He doesn't know anyone here and he's very shy," the messenger replied. "Well, I'll only dance with him if he comes over and asks me," I said, but alas the young man was too shy to ask for himself. It was much later that I discovered that the shy young man was Gerry Dorsey, later to become the singer Englebert Humperdinck. I had turned down the chance to dance with a future pop-star!'

Anne Jones says, 'Everybody knew how to dance the waltz, the quickstep and the foxtrot. The old time favourites like the Palais Glide, the St Bernard's Waltz and the Maxina were always included in the programme. The Palais de Danse was open every night, with its two tier bandstand and non-stop dancing to the Alhambra Players, but Friday night was *the* night to be seen there. On Saturdays, the choice of venues was enormous. Wynns Oriental in the Market Place, Lancaster Hall (with the Johnny Lester band), the De Montfort Hall, Granby Halls, and a miscellany of smaller places such as the Casino, the Empire, the Astoria, all of which gave lessons during the week, followed by two hours of social dancing. Out of town village halls, such as the Kirby Muxloe community centre were all well patronised and usually overcrowded, well into the rock-and-roll era. The *crème de la crème* was the Bell Hotel; it cost six shillings on a Saturday night, but how glorious.

'Theatres too were much in prominence. There was the Theatre Royal in Horsefair Street, home of the repertory company which produced such stars as Billie Whitelaw and Brian Glover. On Monday nights, it was two for the price of one, and a different production every week. The De Montfort Hall annually brought the Carla Rosa opera company for three weeks, with opera at prices the ordinary person could afford. The Palace Theatre attracted well-known acts of infinite variety, while the Opera House reached the height of fantasy with their superb Emile Littler pantomimes. Imagine the thrill of being in the Dress Circle (Grandfather's annual treat) with Peter Pan and Wendy flying over our heads. Amateur drama and operatic societies abounded county-wide, where young people could experience the joy of singing and acting in G&S operettas. Kirby Muxloe Players produced both musicals and plays, and there was the Wycliffe Operatic, Melton Operatic, YMCA Operatic.

'There was certainly no dearth of activities in which to become involved if one so wished. We may not have had much money to throw about, but we were far too occupied in our spare time to even contemplate doing drugs, spraying graffiti, attacking old ladies or stealing cars. Could that have been because of the lack of television?'

Anne's mention of the De Montfort Hall leads me on to the reminiscences of Malcolm O'Shea. Malcolm's father, Cyril, was the entertainments manager at Leicester's De Montfort Hall from 1946 to 1961, and Malcolm worked as a steward there between 1951 and 1970. The many stars who performed there during their time include the Beatles (twice), the Rolling Stones, Tommy

Malcolm O'Shea's prized programme of 1953,
signed by Frank Sinatra.

Steele, Danny Kaye, Joe Loss and his orchestra, Harry Gold and his Pieces of Eight, the D'Oyley Carte company, the New York Symphony Orchestra, the Halle, Mario Lanza, Gigli, and Cliff Richard. Malcolm explains that the reason the De Montfort could afford all the top artists in the Forties, Fifties and Sixties was because its capacity then was 3,500, twice what it is today. His father told him that the acoustics at the hall were so good that the architect who was building London's Festival Hall came to study the design.

In 1953, Malcolm was in the army and about to be sent abroad. In July a big American star was appearing at the De Montfort, and Cyril O'Shea asked him if he would sign a programme for his son who was about to embark for Korea. The star duly obliged, adding a message that he hoped the war would be over before Malcolm arrived. That programme is now among Malcolm's most prized possessions, and when he showed it to me, I read, '*All the best son – I hope it's over before you get there, Frank Sinatra.*' Malcolm tells me that when he arrived in Korea, the war had indeed ended, just going to prove what influence Ol' Blue Eyes really had! Another of Malcolm's memories was of linking arms with other staff and police officers to hold back the screaming girls while the Beatles were performing in 1963. 'That's the first and only time he's had to hold screaming girls back,' his wife chuckled to me.

CHAPTER ELEVEN
SUNDAY SCHOOL AND THE ANNIVERSARY FESTIVAL

Many people who contacted me wrote about their memories of going to Sunday school, most of them mentioning the annual Sunday school anniversary. Margaret Sparrow says, 'I joined the Stanton-under-Bardon Congregational chapel Sunday school when I was four years old. I went on to be a teacher there, and played the organ for the Sunday school until I left the village to get married when I was twenty. There were a few special occasions in the chapel calendar that were looked forward to throughout the year, including Easter, Harvest, and Christmas, when we celebrated with carol singing around the village, pulling an old harmonium on wheels, and ending up at someone's house for hot drinks and mince pies.

Sunday school Anniversary 1947 at Welby Lane Mission, Melton.

Welby Lane Mission in the Forties.

'The highlight of the year was the Anniversary, when the children sat up on a wooden gallery and sang hymns they had been practising for the past six weeks. People came from neighbouring villages to sing anthems with the choir. Everyone had new clothes to wear on the day, and what they looked like was a very well kept secret. During the war, clothes were still on coupons and not easy to purchase, but my mum always managed to come up with something. I know she used to buy second-hand clothes from the market, then wash and iron them to look as good as new. One year, I had a red silk dress as a Christmas present, but I had to wait until the Anniversary in June before I could wear it.

'On the evening before the Anniversary, we would practise going to our places on the gallery, which had been erected the night before by male members of the chapel. First the older scholars would go up to the top row, and so on down to the very young ones at the bottom, boys sitting down one side, girls down the other. There were about 70 of us altogether. At the front was the three-man orchestra, consisting of a cornet, violin and double bass. On the morning of the Anniversary there would be one final practice with the orchestra and organ, then home for dinner. Every year the violin player would come to our house for his dinner, along with other visitors. I don't know how my mother managed to prepare everything in time.

'Dad always came to the evening service. We would sit on the gallery looking for our friends and relations in the congregation. During the service there would be a collection, plates being passed round the congregation. We had to put our collection money on a plate before we went up onto the gallery because children were liable to drop theirs through the steps. Grandma always gave me a sixpence to put in the collection. I had this tied in the corner of my handkerchief, and always had trouble getting it undone. After the service the preacher would announce how much the collection had made. It was great if it was more than the previous year; it was nearly always around £145.

'My mum sang in the choir, which sat on a rostrum near the pulpit, and in later years I joined her. We also sang in quite a few neighbouring chapels at their Anniversaries, walking there as there were no buses on a Sunday and none of us had a car. We would walk back to Stanton afterwards, still singing. On the Saturday after the Anniversary came the Sunday school treat, a day out to either Wicksteed Park or Drayton Manor.'

That was in the 1940s and early 1950s, but the local Anniversaries were still an active part of local life in the 1960s. Judith Thompson of Shepshed writes,

A Sunday school outing to Skeggy, 1946.

'I remember "Sitting Up" at the Belton Street Baptist church Sunday school Anniversary weekend, once a year. We sat at the front of the chapel facing the congregation in white gloves and delicate coloured dresses of starched net with rosebud trimmings and receiving a children's bible story book for good attendance.'

Jean Philps also remembers her early start at her church, and how she later turned her church activities into a source of pocket money and a way of meeting boys! She writes, 'I was born in 1942 in a cottage opposite the church of St Helen in Sharnford. One of my earliest memories is being collected and taken to church by the organist, Joan Brown. I sat on the organ bench beside her and was fascinated by all the stops and keys – a double manual – feet dancing about on the pedals effortlessly producing a glorious sound. I couldn't have been very old, as I remember the bonnets I wore, particularly a green felt one decorated with little flowers. I think that early introduction to church life stood me in good stead, as I am still an active member of St Helen's.

'We all went to Sunday school, which was held in the large classroom. Each week we were issued with a pretty stamp, which we stuck onto an attendance card. The class was full to overflowing and we learned all about the characters of the bible. No one ever moaned about having to go – it was part of village life.

'Some years later, Harry Wood and his son Jim taught me the art of handbell-ringing. There were five of us, including Harry's granddaughter, Margaret. We soon became competent enough to handle the bells and started to ring with the rest of the band for Sunday services. We had moved on from Sunday school and now spent the afternoons up the Fosse Fields – not to observe nature, but to meet up with the lads from surrounding villages! We would hear the single church bell ringing which meant we had fifteen minutes to get back over the fields for 6 pm. We dare not be late. There was no sneaking out after ringing; we were expected to attend the service. As most of us were in the choir, which we enjoyed, this was no hardship. We were each paid 5/- for ringing at weddings and there seemed plenty of those in the 50s and 60s.'

CHAPTER TWELVE
DAN DARE, DICK BARTON AND THE GOON SHOW

M any children read the *Dandy* and the *Beano* at an early stage of their life, following the misdeeds of Lord Snooty, Desperate Dan and Korky the Cat. There was also a comic called *Radio Fun*, where all the strip cartoons were based on characters we heard on the wireless: Arthur Askey ('The Little Man With The Big Heart'), Peter Brough and Archie Andrews, Cardew Robinson ('Cardew the Cad'). Then, in 1950, a new comic was launched: The *Eagle*. As a response to the import of American horror and crime comics, a young clergyman called Marcus Morris decided to create a comic that would be – as he saw it – more wholesome.

The first *Eagle* was published on 14th April 1950. It cost 3d, and eight of its twenty pages were in full colour. The front cover (and page two) were devoted to the adventures of Colonel Dan Dare, Pilot of the Future. This clean-cut astronaut fought the evil Treens, green people from Mars, and their leader the Mekon. (My friend, Alistair Treen had a hard time of it, sharing a name with the villains of the piece.) The Mekon had a large head and a small body, whereas Dan Dare was very athletic and heroic. I think psychologists would probably see an underlying message to beware of becoming too intellectual; the ethos of The *Eagle* was one of muscular Christianity. This story was created by artist Frank Hampson and became the *Eagle*'s most famous feature.

The back page story was about the life of St Paul, reflecting the Christian ethos of the *Eagle*. Later back page series included the life and adventures of David

Dan Dare's exploits in the Eagle *were closely followed by children everywhere.*

Livingstone, Baden-Powell and Winston Churchill, though I'm not sure how the latter fitted into the back page religious slot. One of the *Eagle*'s special features was the centre spread which showed cut-away drawings of ships, planes, trains, cars, weapons, etc. These diagrams covered the upper half of the two centre pages, and many boys – the *Eagle* was undeniably aimed at boys – cut them out and stuck them on their bedroom walls. Derek Whitmore of Whitwick, who still has a collection of the Dan Dare stories from the first year of the *Eagle*, says 'In the good old days of the Fifties, our pin-ups were aeroplanes and trains rather than scantily clad women!'

Other stories in the *Eagle* featured *Riders of the Range*, the adventures of cowboy Jeff Arnold, created by Charles Chiltern, *Luck of the Legion* (based on the French Foreign Legion), and *PC 49* (based on a radio series of the same name). Humorous comic strips included *Captain Pugwash*, later to become a television series, and *Harris Tweed*, a bumbling Special Agent. One of the strips was a commercially sponsored story, featuring a boy called Tommy Walls, whose super powers were invoked by him making a W sign with his hands. This strip was sponsored by Walls Ice Cream.

The advertisements in the *Eagle* are quite interesting: Stanley Matthews Football Boots and Kodak camera film adverts were next to enrolment forms urging boys to join the Royal Navy.

Cowboy Jeff Arnold of the Eagle was another firm favourite.

Joe Booth of Braunston reminds me that the editorials were written by the Rev Marcus Morris. Boys were encouraged to send in stories about friends who did good deeds, performed with no expectation of reward. These heroes received badges shaped like mugs, since, the editor argued, people would call them mugs for doing things for others. It was better to be a 'mug', the theory ran, than the opposite: a spiv. Joe doesn't think the mug badges concept lasted very long, but readers were also encouraged to join the Eagle Club and received a metal badge in the shape of an eagle. I was thrilled to be able to obtain Frank Hampson's autograph, and also that of Frank Humphris, the artist behind *Riders of the Range*. Strangely the latter signed it as Jeff Arnold, one of the characters, though he did add a drawing with his signature.

At about this time (1953), I was confined to bed for eight weeks with a serious illness. A friend of my father lent me a book called *Swallows and Amazons* by Arthur Ransome. I devoured this, and then read book after book by this author. Some were set in the Lake District, others on the Norfolk Broads. I decided that sailing was the thing for me, and my sickbed became a boat! When I recovered from my illness, my new ambition was to join the Navy. Although I changed my mind about the direction of my life, my friend Johnny Wingett – a fellow Navy enthusiast – went ahead with his decision and signed up. He rose through the ranks to become a Petty Officer. The last I heard of him – surprisingly on *This Is Your Life* – he had become a Lieutenant. (The programme was actually about the life of his son Mark, an actor in *The Bill*.)

In 1949 we were beginning to be persuaded not to 'make do' any longer.

Our main means of entertainment in those pre-television days was the radio (or the wireless, as we called it). A childhood favourite of mine was *Dick Barton, Special Agent*, an adventure serial featuring the hero of the title. This fifteen-minute programme was broadcast every day at 6.45 pm. I must have been quite young when I started listening because I recall that I had to go to bed as soon as the programme finished at seven o'clock. In the south of the county Jean Philps was listening too. She comments, '*Dick Barton, Special Agent* was a must on the wireless. At a quarter to seven, mum would shout, "It's on!" – as mums all over the country probably did, and the street emptied as we all ran in for the next exciting episode of Dick, Snowy and Jock.' I thought it was a very bad move when the BBC replaced Dick Barton with a serial called *The Archers*. 'This will never last,' I announced knowledgeably. 'Who will want to listen to a story about a bunch of farmers?' Ah. The wisdom of youth.

Another programme I recall was *Have A Go*, a quiz show run by Wilfred and Mabel Pickles, who would travel to different towns and interview local people. If he had a child on the show, Wilfred would always embarrass him by asking, 'Are you courting?' Other catchphrases included 'How much on the table, Mabel?' and 'Give him the money, Barney' which seemed hilarious to us at the time. *ITMA* (which stood for It's That Man Again) was another comedy favourite, and featured Tommy Handley. Catchphrases from that show were Jack Train's 'I don't mind if I do' referring to his misinterpreting innocent remarks as an invitation to have a drink, and also the miserable charlady, Mona Lott, saying 'It's being so cheerful that keeps me going.'

In my teens, I became a fan of *The Goon Show*. This radio programme, featuring Peter Sellers, Spike Milligan, Harry Secombe and Michael Bentine, was loathed by our parents ('I can't see the point of it! What is it supposed to mean?'), but this made it all the more popular with us. We could do all the voices of the characters, and would produce the catchphrases at any opportunity. At school, one of the best imitators of the various Goon characters was a lad called Graham Chapman, who later found comedy fame himself when he became one of the Monty Python team and starred in films like *The Life of Brian*.

Mavis Wright of Market Harborough says that she 'loved listening to radio plays, especially *Saturday Night Theatre* and *The Man In Black*, a series of scary plays, introduced by Valentine Dyall. Any creepy plays were best listened to in the dark,' she claims.

In the Sixties, of course, we deserted the radio for the television and became addicts of the new cop-shows like *Z Cars*, and its successor *Softly, Softly*, but

the radio still holds some advantages over its new and brasher competitor.
Maurice Keightley of Leicester Forest East explains: 'Even today, I am a great
fan of the radio. Radio plays are somehow more atmospheric than those on
television, because we provide the visual details ourselves. The scenery is more
picturesque and the girls are definitely much prettier!'

POSTSCRIPT

The one thing that has emerged from my researches into the period of 1939-69 is the change of lifestyle covered by the three decades. In music, the era begins with Vera Lynn singing *We'll Meet Again*, a sentiment devoutly wished by all the listeners separated by the war, and ends with the Beatles singing *Hey Jude* and the Rolling Stones serenading their *Honkey Tonk Women*. In between came the folk club scene, the traditional jazz revival, and the rock'n'roll Fifties. At the cinema, we began by watching the romantic *Gone With The Wind* and *The Philadelphia Story*, soon followed by heroic war films like *We Dive At Dawn* and *In Which We Serve*. By the end of the period, it was the more sophisticated fare of *Midnight Cowboy* and *The Graduate* that entertained us.

In our home life, the Forties found us huddling round a coal fire, with some people taking their weekly bath in front of that same fire, whereas by 1969 central heating was making life more comfortable and making it possible for us to enjoy the whole house, even in winter! In the Forties, most of us took the eleven-plus exam to decide whether we would go to a grammar school or a secondary modern. By the end of the Sixties, the whole of Leicestershire had a comprehensive system, under which decisions about higher education could be made at a later age than eleven.

Holidays – virtually unknown during the war years – usually meant a week in Skeggy in the post-war Forties, whereas by the end of the period people were looking to foreign travel and Spanish beaches that were less bracing than those of England's east coast!

For people of my generation – I was born in 1939 – the period of this book transported us from one world into a very different one.

ACKNOWLEDGEMENTS

I would like to express my thanks to BBC Radio Leicester and to the local newspapers which carried my appeal for contributions, including the *Leicester Mail* series, the *Leicester Mercury*, the *Melton Times*, the *Loughborough Echo* series, the *Market Harborough Mail*, the *Hinckley Times*, and the *Ashby Times*. Melton Carnegie Museum, Barton Transport and Leicestershire & Rutland County WI all gave me help and useful information.

Most of all I am grateful for the many individuals who loaned me photographs and gave me their reminiscences of Leicestershire in the Forties, Fifties and Sixties. I couldn't use everything I received, but I thank everyone whether their material was used or not. These individuals include: Jean and Herbert Allison, Peggy Andrews, Delia Bennett, Ron Bignell, Frank Bingley, Pauline Black, Joe Booth, Jean Bowes, John Brooks, Molly Carter, Terence C. Cartwright, Sally Choice, Nellie Clarke (and her friend Grace), Jenny Dancey, Jill Driver, Joan Ecob, Mark Ferrelly, John A. Green, Pat Hall, Grizelda Hargreaves, Rosemary Heyes, Stella James, Betty Johnson, Margaret Johnson, Shaun Johnson, Anne Jones, Arnold Jordan, Maurice Keightley, David Kyle, Brian McNeill, Kay Moon, Phyllis Morgan, Ann Musson, Malcolm O'Shea, Jean Philps, Margaret Pick, Mary Punter, Elizabeth Riding, Chick Rushton, Steve Sharp, Mrs M.R. Shorley, Anne Silins, Margaret Sparrow, Joyce Smith, Joyce Swift, Judith Thompson, Stuart Warburton, John Whitaker, Derek Whitehouse, Derek Whitmore, Mavis Wright, Mary Yendall, and 'Fred' from Wigston.